How to
CREATE YOUR

OWN PUBLICITY

FOR NAMES, PRODUCTS OR SERVICES
AND GET IT FOR
FREE

How To
CREATE YOUR
OWN PUBLICITY
FOR NAMES, PRODUCTS
OR SERVICES AND GET IT FOR
FREE

STEVE BERMAN

Fell's Books Fill Your Needs

FREDERICK FELL PUBLISHERS, INC.
New York

Library of Congress Cataloging In Publication Data

Berman, Steve.
    How to create your own publicity for names, products,
or services, and get it for free.

    1. Pulicity. 2. Public relations. I. Title.
HM263.B392   659.2   77-2736
ISBN 0-8119-0287-0
ISBN 0-88391-062-4 pbk.

For information address:

Frederick Fell Publishers, Inc.
386 Park Avenue South
New York, New York 10016

Published Simultaneously in Canada by:
Thomas Nelson & Sons, Limited
Don Mills, Ontario, Canada

1 2 3 4 5 6 7 8 9 0

MANUFACTURED IN THE UNITED STATES OF AMERICA

Designed by Michael U. Polvere

WITH SPECIAL THANKS TO...

Sheldon Aronwitz
Jean Bach
Gwen Barrett
Jeff Berman
Peter Faris
Arlene Francis
Joe Franklin
Amy Goldberg
Donna Gould
John Koster
R. Allen Leider
Mike Levine
Jim Lord
Alec Nagle
Gail North
Mimi O'Brien
Penny Price
Emil Romano
Jane Salek
Lannie Spalding
Miriam Stewart
Peter Wesselton
Hal Wingo

CONTENTS

INTRODUCTION

This book tells what publicity is, how it works, and how easy it is to do. In short—everything you need to know to become your own successful publicist, while saving countless thousands of dollars normally paid to a professional.

Publicity is the art of communicating your message to the public. It is the one form of advertising which is FREE.

Over the years many people have come to me seeking help and advice on various publicity projects, thinking of me as a "God-like" creature holding the power and influence needed to convey their message to the world. Most of these people are disappointed to learn that they cannot afford to pay for my professional services. So what are these people to do? The only thing they can do—they can do their *own* publicity. That is the aim of this book. To teach those of you who need publicity but can't afford the exhorbitant fees charged, how to do it yourself.

Whether you're promoting a product, person, service or idea, publicity is your free key to success and recognition. A few examples of how doing your own publicity will pay off are: the singer, musician, actor or actress who knows the right T.V. exposure will bring them the break they've been waiting for; the independent author who feels public awareness will insure a best-seller; the restauranteur who can't afford the high cost of paid advertising; the inventor with a terrific idea who thinks he can make a million if people only knew about his product; or the public servant, politician, doctor, lawyer, non-profit or charitable organization promoting a cause, theory, or service. Whatever their reasons, all of these people and millions just like them have one thing in common—the need for publicity.

Anybody who is enthusiastic and bright can accomplish what a first-class publicist can, thus enabling them to achieve their desired goals and recognition. Throughout these pages, you will find the necessary tools, fundamentals, practical and proven methods for you to learn, step by step, how simple it is to become a master in the art of publicity.

CHAPTER 1

DEFINING THE PUBLICITY PROCESS

WHAT IS PUBLICITY?

Congratulations! You've decided to learn how to do your own publicity. This is probably one of the most important decisions you will ever make. Once you learn how to use publicity, you'll understand why it's a sure-fire method in winning success for your ideas, ambitions, service, or product.

Before teaching you how publicity works, we must first define what publicity is. If you want to publicize or promote a product, service or idea, you can buy an ad in your local newspaper, or pay for a radio or TV commercial, if you can afford the cost. But is this publicity? No, this is advertising... paying for time and space. Advertising costs money.

Then what is publicity? Simply stated, publicity means bringing your message to the public's attention without having to pay for the exposure.

So, what does a store owner do if he wishes to call attention to his wares, but can't afford the high cost of buying a commercial message on a local radio or TV show? How does the teacher, disgusted with deplorable conditions within the

15

school system, voice his frustrations without taking out and paying for a full-page ad in the local paper? What does a newly established clothes designer do to win recognition for her unique creations without having to spend a large amount of money purchasing ad space in a top fashion magazine? On the other hand, how can an actor waiting for his big break achieve fame without paying for the professional services of a publicity agent?

The answer to all of these questions is simple. These people can all learn how to do their own publicity and get their desired recognition for free. That's right, absolutely free!

Publicity enables a person to achieve success without costing a cent. It is a myth to believe that you must spend large sums of money to reach a large audience. This couldn't be further from the truth. A shrewd and knowledgeable publicist, if what he says has importance or is of interest, does not have to pay for his message to be heard.

THE MASS MEDIA

The best and most powerful way of attaining success and conveying your message to the largest audience is by using the mass media. What is meant by mass media? The mass media are television, radio, magazines and newspapers, our world's communications network. The sooner you learn how the mass media operates and how to operate within it, the sooner you will be on the road to success.

Today, we live in a competitive world. To exist, you must know how to compete within it. It's just not enough to have a good idea. You must also learn how to market your idea. And this is what I intend to teach you...how to successfully market yourself, your idea, product or cause.

YOU AND THE MEDIA—EQUAL PARTNERS

People in the media need you just as much as you need them. Without news, interesting people and human interest stories, magazines and newspapers would go out of business, and many radio and TV shows would go off the air. Good guests and stories do not just materialize out of thin air. Good guests and stories must be found. *You* can become that interesting or unusual story if you learn what the media looks for.

Developing an honest and close working relationship with media personnel is essential. Your contacts are worth their weight in gold. Your ideas must be well thought out, well-timed and planned, to merit free space and time available in the print and broadcast medias. In gearing your campaign, you must learn to have a nose for news, and what will sell.

Ideas are usually presented in three ways. Either your idea is a general news item, unique or off-beat, or of human interest.

A woman voicing her objections to the closing of the only fire station in her neighborhood because of a lack of funds would be an example of a general news story. A singing chicken would be a classic example of your unique or off-beat story. The restauranteur who opens his doors once a week to anyone over 65 in need of a free meal, is an example of a human interest story.

The above examples are typical of stories and ideas offered to the media every day. And if your story idea is accepted, you not only get the publicity *you* want, but you're giving the media a story *they* want. It's a case of one hand washing the other.

PUBLICITY—YOUR PART-TIME ENDEAVOR

It is not my intention to teach you how to be a full-time professional publicist even though I believe it can be one of the most rewarding careers available to a bright and creative person. Rather, I would like you to learn to become a part-time professional, knowing when and how to effectively use the media to your advantage whenever the need for publicity may arise. Your publicity efforts will pay off only after learning the basic techniques. It is then that you become a part-time master in the art of publicity.

BUILDING YOUR "ANGLE"

Before launching a publicity campaign you must first decide what it is you are trying to say, and whether people will be interested in what you are saying. You must determine who and where your audiences are, and how best to reach them. Each day, millions of people are bombarded by messages and information when switching on their television sets and radios, and when purchasing newspapers and magazines at their local newsstands. People demand to be entertained and informed on matters which effect the way they think and live. People are starved for all kinds of information, so if you can fill their appetite for news, you've succeeded in your task...acquiring your publicity...for free.

But what if you determine, after analyzing your idea, that your message lacks interest or is not needed? Then what do you do? You must gear your angle differently to create an interest or need.

Getting back to our unknown actor friend who is seeking fame and recognition; he finds it extremely tough to get his first break. Most talk shows and newspapers refuse him time because he is one of many unknown actors. So, he must think up another approach to get himself the coverage he seeks. One example which would insure him of getting the publicity he needs would be for him to volunteer his services and time to teaching handicapped youngsters how to communicate through acting. He has now found his newsworthy angle, and it will be easy for him to get his publicity.

The actor has achieved three major accomplishments: he gets his publicity; he has set himself apart from other aspiring actors, and, beside helping himself, he was able to help others also in need. So obviously, where there is a will, there is a way. You can sell any idea as long as you can come up with an interesting or newsworthy angle. Remember, your main concern always should be that what you are promoting is of interest or need to those persons you are trying to reach.

THE VALUE AND BENEFITS OF PUBLICITY

Everyone wants as much free publicity as he can get. Who

wouldn't want a front page story? Who wouldn't want the entire hour to himself on a local TV talk show? This would be ideal, but it's not always the case.

Think of it this way. Let's say it costs $200 for a one-minute paid advertisement on a local t.v. show. You are invited on that same show as a guest, and given five minutes on the air. If you were to equate how much that same five minutes would have cost you if you were paying for that time, you would arrive at a figure of $1,000. Think about that. You received $1,000 worth of free publicity.

Let's look at another example of the monetary value of free publicity. An artist is seeking publicity for his gallery. He knows it will cost him at least $500 for a one-half page ad in a well-circulated local newspaper. He can't afford this cost, so he must think up an angle to get himself free publicity. After giving the matter considerable thought, he plans his strategy. He manages, on his own, to get a free one-half page article printed about himself. The article that appears in the paper is a feature story about the artist's hobby. His hobby, painting animals which are endangered species, was his idea for getting publicity for his gallery. It was a good idea because it worked. Not only did his story get a big space in the paper, but his picture, pictures of some of his paintings, and the name and location of his gallery were also mentioned. See what a little ingenuity can do? The artist not only received the publicity he wanted, but saved $500 in the process. His story was probably seen and read by more people than if it would have appeared as an advertisement.

Always be happy with any type of publicity you can get, even if it's only a one-minute radio interview or a brief mention in the paper. Any form of publicity is a gift in itself. Remember, you are not the one who decides how much time and space you'll get. That decision is up to the producer or editor.

Some shows have better reputations than others. Formats differ, as do audiences. However the golden rule of publicity is...THE BEST SHOW IS THE ONE YOU GET ON—THE BEST PAPER IS THE ONE YOU GET IN. No matter how small the show or paper may be, all forms of broadcast and print media have value. You never know who might be watching the show or reading the paper which you consider unimportant.

Now that you understand what publicity is, and what it can do for you, you're ready to learn how to properly develop and execute a successful publicity campaign. Your next step is preparing the press kit.

CHAPTER 2

THE PRESS KIT

THE PRESS KIT AND ITS IMPORTANCE

The press kit is a package of written material which tells about you, your idea or service. It is sent to TV and radio producers and to newspaper and magazine editors in hopes that they will like your idea and thus publicize your story.

Media personnel will rarely agree to interview you or write about your story without first seeing your press kit. The old line, "send me the information," usually holds true. Your press kit must speak for you! It must tell your story!

You don't have to be a professional writer to be able to prepare and write your press kit. If you are enthusiastic and can clearly state your idea verbally, then it will be just as easy for you to express your idea on paper.

A properly prepared press kit includes the release, background sheet, suggested questions, newspaper clips and photos. Once written and organized, all of this information is then placed into a folder and sent to those shows and periodicals where you seek publicity.

THE GENERAL RELEASE

The release is usually a one or sometimes two page informative story which gives important facts about the person, subject or idea being publicized. The release should be loaded with facts; the main selling point of the story should be described in the opening sentence. Additional information supporting the story is written in subsequent paragraphs. A release must be well-organized, giving a constant and smooth flow of information. Your name and phone number must appear on the release so that a producer or reporter can contact you if interested in your story, or if they need further information. Also, include the dates you are available to be interviewed.

As stated in Chapter 1, publicity ideas are usually presented in one of three ways. Either your idea is a general news item, unique or off-beat, or it's of human interest. Let's now look at the three releases given as examples on the following pages, and observe styles and "angles."

The Press Kit

RELEASE #1
GENERAL NEWS STORY

James Patrick, prominent astrologer, has predicted that a woman will be elected President in next year's election.

This, his latest forecast, pertains to a woman who is now quite active in New York politics.

"The pattern of the stars indicates that this woman will inevitably be elected President of the United States."

Mr. Patrick's predictions can't easily be disregarded. In recent years he accurately predicted the Watergate scandal, the Patty Hearst kidnap, and three major airline crashes.

Many persons who were before skeptical, and joked about Mr. Patrick's prophecies, aren't laughing anymore. His forecasts are taken so seriously that the local police department recently hired him to help locate a young girl who had been missing for two weeks. The result—he found her!

CONTACT: MR. JAMES PATRICK
201 HAMILTON ST.
ANYWHERE, U.S.A.
(208) 952-6782

RELEASE #2
UNIQUE OFF-BEAT STORY

The world's largest all-girl band has been formed.

Famed bandleader Elsa Freelander scoured the country for 10 long months finding the oddest and most talented female musicians to play in her band. The band, called She-Nah, has 47 female members. The group plays every sound imaginable, from Bach to the Beatles.

Every instrument you can imagine can be heard while listening to She-Nah, including the sounds of 17 guitars, three sets of drums, bongos, organs and clarinets. Another unique feature of the band is that all the women wear cheetah loin cloth costumes.

These swinging gals are really a novelty. They can presently be heard at Omar's Restaurant, on Park Avenue.

FOR FURTHER INFORMATION CONTACT: DONALD OMAR
(212) 997-0984

RELEASE #3
HUMAN INTEREST STORY

Mr. and Mrs. John Drake, former welfare recipients, are now millionaires!

For most of their lives, the Drakes lived on a shoestring budget. Mr. Drake is an invalid, paralyzed from the legs down. After suffering from a freak accident 5 years ago, he found it virtually impossible to get a job. Mrs. Drake, besides caring for her 11 children, did a little sewing on the side to make some extra money. Between welfare assistance and the small amounts of money Mrs. Drake earned each week, the family somehow managed to get by.

But being a proud and enterprising man, wanting to give his children those things in life which he never had, Mr. Drake asked his wife to teach him how to sew clothes. And that was the beginning of the Drake success story.

Working out of their small apartment, the Drakes took old clothing that their children had outgrown and fixed them up. They then sold these recycled garments to friends and neighbors who couldn't afford the price of new clothes. In a short time, Mr. Drake's idea turned into a real money-making business.

That was 15 years ago. Today Mr. and Mrs. Drake are the proud owners of the Oldies But Goodies Clothes Shop on Market Street, the world's largest used clothing store. They also now own a 20-room mansion in the suburbs.

That's the sad story with a happy ending. A story of a family that went from rags to riches!

CONTACT: JOHN DRAKE
          923-0865

EXPLANATIONS

Release number one is an example of a news story. The astrologer, to set himself apart from other astrologers, in his hunger for publicity, couldn't lose by making such a sensational prediction. The first woman President is definitely news and the astrologer knew it. He could get all the free publicity he wants with that prediction.

The second release is an example of your unique type story...the world's largest all-girl band. In an effort to cash in on free publicity for his eatery, the owner of Omar's thought up this terrific angle to call attention to his restaurant. He hires an all-girl band to perform, and then publicizes this unique attraction.

Release number three is of human interest, a story capable of reaching the hearts of millions of people. Mr. Drake is a shrewd businessman. He's cashing in on his past poverty by still turning rags into riches. He will be able to obtain free publicity for his clothing store with this tear-jerker story.

You will notice that all three releases used as examples are short, to the point, interesting and state the story's main point in the first sentence.

When writing your release, use any style of writing you feel most comfortable with. You can even write a humorous release if the occasion calls for it. So have fun. Don't ever be afraid to experiment with your ideas.

(NOTE: An entire press kit is not needed if you merely wish to have an announcement about a certain event appear in your local paper.) Examples would be wedding announcements, club meetings and charity events. What is needed, though, is a special "press release" which should be sent to local newspapers for printing. This type of "press release" is constructed differently from the types described in this chapter, and will be covered in detail in Chapter 5.

The Press Kit

THE BACKGROUND SHEET

The background sheet, or fact sheet, backgrounder, or resume, as it is otherwise called, simply lists any additional story information deemed important which was not already mentioned in the release.

If you're promoting a product, service or idea, you would give any added facts by listing them on the background sheet as 1., 2., 3., etc., with a brief sentence or two for each numbered fact.

Let's use as an example our "all-girl" orchestra talked about earlier. The restaurant owner who is preparing the press kit might use the background sheet to mention some of the more unusual instruments played in the band, or list some interesting background facts about a few of the girls, in hopes of enhancing the story and making it more appealing. Anything that might add to a story's importance or interest, not otherwise mentioned, or only briefly written about in the release, should be used in the background sheet.

Another example of the background sheet's purpose would be for the individual who is seeking publicity where it pertains to his profession. Let's say a lawyer is seeking publicity for a case he is handling, or a doctor wishes the world to know about a new medical breakthrough he has devised. Naturally, the publicity these men wants pertains to their professions. Before any media representatives would cover these stories, they would first want to see some background information on these men, or resumes listing their professional qualifications. The media seeks this information merely to establish credibily. The lawyer's and doctor's resumes should be included within their press kits. Their resumes should include information about where they attended college, degrees received, and where they currently practice.

SUGGESTED QUESTIONS FOR YOUR INTERVIEWER

Suggested questions are written by you for the interviewer to ask. These suggested questions are part of your press kit.

How To Create Your Own Publicity

Talk show hosts and reporters usually have little free time to prepare questions to ask you in advance, even though they probably have familiarized themselves with your story and know basically what they will ask you. By offering media people your suggested questions in advance, you're helping them by making their job easier and simultaneously helping yourself.

There are two major benefits in writing your own suggested questions. First, you know in advance the questions that the interviewer is likely to ask, so you can prepare your answers in advance. Secondly, by writing your own questions, you can gear the discussion to those points and issues *you* wish to primarily talk about.

But always be prepared and ready for an interviewer to throw you some zingers by coming up with a few questions of his own. This is especially true when your story pertains to a controversial issue. Since astrology, for example, isn't a proven science, and is a controversial subject, our astrologer, Mr. Patrick, might be thrown some unexpected derogatory or negative questions by a talk show host non-believer. You must always be alert and on your toes, if your publicity idea is controversial in nature.

The following example lists suggested questions which Mr. Patrick, the astrologer, might use.

SAMPLE: A SUGGESTED QUESTION SHEET

Suggested Questions For James Patrick, Astrologer

1. How long have you practiced astrology?

2. How would you define astrology?

3. People today really seem to be into each others "signs." Is this sudden interest in astrology merely a fad?

4. Are people now taking astrology more seriously?

5. Is there any well-known astrologer today who you would consider a "quack?"

6. How long before the Hearst kidnap and the Watergate scandel, two incidents which you accurately predicted, did you foresee these events taking place?

7.Did you ever sense a tragedy was to occur and report your feelings to the police?

8. You have predicted that next year, a woman, active in New York politics, will be elected President. How did you predict this?

You should always prepare at least six or seven suggested questions. They should be short and to the point. Your questions should reflect upon the most interesting and important points of your story. They should be the type of questions you would like to hear asked of a person being interviewed on TV or in the newspaper.

NEWSPAPER CLIPS AND PHOTOS

If there have ever been any newspaper or magazine articles written about you or your publicity ideas, it's a good idea to enclose mimeographed copies of these stories in your press kit. Obviously, they will help add to your story's and your importance. If you're just starting out, and there has never been a story printed about you, don't be concerned. If the story that you wish to publicize has importance and interest, you will still get the publicity that you're after.

It is always a good idea to include a picture of yourself in your press kit. A picture, as the saying goes, "is worth a thousand words." and always adds personal warmth to any press kit submitted for consideration.

You might also want to include additional pictures which might intensify the interest in your story and give it more appeal. Mr. Drake, the "old clothes" store owner, might be wise to include pictures of his old run-down apartment and the 20-room mansion he lives in today, to show in pictures a before-and-after look.

To sum up, your completed press kit should include a release, background sheet, suggested questions, newspaper clips if available, and photos. Once your press kit is prepared you're ready for that big moment...appearing on TV, being interviewed on radio, and in newspapers and magazines...you're ready now to grab your free publicity!

CHAPTER 3

MAKING THE BIG TIME

THE PUBLICITY CAMPAIGN—PLAN YOUR STRATEGY: MAKE YOUR MOVE

What are your reasons for seeking publicity? Is it the desire for fame? Fortune? Calling attention to yourself or your group? Maybe a combination of all of the above?

No matter why your interest in publicity, planning a proper publicity campaign can help insure you of receiving the recognition you expect and deserve.

Think about your favorite actor or celebrity for a moment. Think about how many articles you have read recently about this person, how often you've heard the name pop up in a conversation or mentioned on TV and radio, and you'll better understand the value and importance of publicity and what it can do.

Those of you who are store owners, business people, sales people, teachers, doctors, housewives, lawyers, politicans, policemen, students, members of religious, charity or school groups, and the like, are primarily interested in getting publicity on a local level.

You are interested in reaching those people in your own community who have an interest in what you are saying. A man seeking publicity for his liquor store in Miami, Florida, doesn't care about reaching people living in Bismark, North Dakota. He only cares about reaching prospective customers in the Miama area.

There are also those of you interested in using publicity on a larger scale to launch a career. If you're an actor, actress, comedian, musician, dancer, writer, artist or inventor, not only are you interested in local publicity but also in regional and national publicity.

No matter what category you fall into, begin building your publicity campaign on a local level. Once you achieve local credibility it's much easier to expand your boundaries. Time, coupled with perseverance and agressiveness will enable you to reach your ultimate goals.

WHAT SHOWS AND PUBLICATIONS ARE FOR YOU?

No matter where you live, there are probably newspapers, radio stations and television stations nearby. But which ones are for you?

There's only one way to find out; do a little research. It won't take long and it will definitely pay off.

Let's use TV as an example. If you're an avid television fan, you know that not all the shows you watch are produced where you live. Some are produced in other parts of the country and aired on your local stations. If you are unsure about which TV and radio shows are produced in your area, the best thing to do is call the station and speak either to the program director or someone in the program department. They can furnish you with this information. After you find out which shows originate from your area, watch and listen to them to study their formats. Which shows accept guests? What types of guests do they put on? Learn what each show looks for in a guest, so you can decide which to be on. (Listings of all TV and radio stations in your area are normally in the TV/radio section of your newspaper, but if not, check your local Yellow Pages for complete listings.)

Now to the newspapers. Pick up copies of all local newspapers known to you, study their writing styles and the types of stories printed. See if they print articles similar to what you have in mind. Check if they use pictures for support, and if there's a special day of the week certain story types are printed. It's also a good idea to visit your local library to find out if there are any other print media in your area that you are unaware of, and which might offer you additional publicity outlets.

Never be swayed by anyone who tells you that a certain TV show, radio show or newspaper is not "good enough" or worth the time to contact. As discussed in Chapter 1, any form of publicity is valuable, and adds credibility to your name or cause.

WHO TO CONTACT—THE NAME OF THE GAME

You know now what shows you would like to appear on and what newspapers interest you. So it's time to find out who is responsible for booking guests and setting up interviews.

For television and radio shows, simply call and ask who books the show. Generally, on larger TV and radio shows, this job belongs to the producer, associate producer or talent coordinator. On smaller shows, the program or news director will generally book guests, or the emcees themselves.

Newspapers are run a little differently. If you are working with a larger paper, a specific editor should be contacted. For example, let's say you're promoting a unique restaurant where the customer orders by computer. Immediately you have three good angles to go on which would make a nice feature story. Your story could be developed nicely into a food, business or science feature. You might want to go first to the food editor. But what if the food editor says no to your idea? Don't give up so quickly. Next go to the science editor and try to interest him. And what about the business editor?

Another example would be a clothes manufacturer who designs unusual swimsuits. This person might first try to interest the woman's editor, or maybe the fashion editor might like the idea. If you think hard, I'll bet you can find at least two or three different angles for your story idea.

With smaller newspapers, it is generally the city editors who make story assignments. Smaller papers don't always have editors who specialize in given areas but do have general assignment reporters. To save time and energy when dealing with a small paper, go directly to the City Editor. If he's interested in your story, he will assign a reporter to cover it.

THE PHONE CALL OR "PITCH"

Now that you know who to contact, you're ready to make your phone call to "pitch" your story.

Before calling, practice what you intend to say. Producers

and editors, are busy and have little time to talk on the phone for long periods of time.

It might sometimes be difficult reaching certain contacts. Producers and editors, besides working their shows and preparing their papers, have meetings and conferences throughout the day and are not always in, nor available for phone calls. So if you don't get through the first time, be patient and keep on trying. In the long run, your efforts will pay off. Also, never call a producer when you know his show is taping, or about to go on the air live.

When you get through to your party, be enthusiastic, and make your story sound interesting and exciting. Make this feeling rub off on the person you're speaking with. Make him feel the excitement. But if the editor or producer seems to turn off to what you are saying, be prepared to offer another angle for your story.

One thing to keep in mind is that the larger the market, the tougher it can be to get a booking. For example, it is generally more difficult to get a booking in New York, Chicago and Los Angeles, because programs and papers in these cities are deluged every day with interesting story ideas and guests. In smaller markets across the country where there aren't as many guests available, it is usually easier to arrange an interview. But remember, no matter how large or small a show or paper may be, if your story is of interest, you've got just as good a chance as anyone else to get an interview.

SENDING THE PRESS KIT

If a producer or editor on a smaller show or paper is interested in your story, he might agree to an interview while speaking to you on the phone. But in order to learn a little more about you, and to prepare himself for the interview, he will probably ask you to send some information about the story. On larger shows and newspapers, contacts will most likely ask you to send this information before giving you an answer. This is where your press kit, discussed in Chapter 2, comes in.

When requested, send out your prepared press kit and wait a few days until you are sure that it had time to arrive and the producer or editor has had a chance to look over it. When you send your press kit, also attach a short covering letter reminding the contact of your phone call and that you have enclosed the material which he requested. It's a good idea to put your name and phone number on the covering letter, because even though it appears on the press release, busy producers and editors sometimes don't have the time to read through all the material you send.

THE FOLLOW-UP CALL—GET THAT BOOKING!

Never sit back and wait for your contacts to get back in touch with you, even though many times they will if interested in your story. Go on the assumption that 100 other people are also waiting for calls on story ideas. You must be aggressive to get ahead. It sometimes might take many calls for a contact to give you a yes or no answer, but just stay patient. Never worry about "bugging" people, or making a pest of yourself. Be aggressive but be diplomatic too. Remember they need you just as much as you need them. Even if you get a "no," thank the person for their time and say you'll be back in touch with other ideas. Be polite and never become nasty. You may need these people again later on.

Don't become discouraged if you get a "no." It doesn't necessarily mean that someone didn't like your idea. Perhaps the show or paper had no available space or time. The same contact who turned you down this time might accept another story idea another time. The best pros in the business expect to get, and do get, turn-downs. It's part of the publicity game.

Another point to notice is that some shows want an exclusive on a story, or want the guest first. The same holds true with newspapers. A few of the most popular programs and papers might only agree to do an interview if they get to do it first and sometimes exclusively. If this should happen, you must weigh the situation carefully. You will have to decide which is worth more, that particular interview, or a combination of many others.

PRE-SHOW INTERVIEWS

A few of the top-rated TV and radio shows throughout the country like to interview prospective guests before agreeing to an appearance. They do this to protect themselves against guests who might sound great over the phone, but do not come across well on the air. If a show asks that you come down for a chat, do it. It means that they're interested in you.

THE CONFIRMATION

After a show or newspaper agrees to a booking or interview, I would suggest sending the contact a letter of confirmation. A letter of confirmation is merely a note confirming that they have agreed to use you or your story, and that you will be there the day and time agreed upon.

THE ITINERARY

I think it's also a good idea to make yourself an itinerary, which is a list of all your appointments. An itinerary is for your own personal use, and lists contact names, times, addresses, dates, and phone numbers for all the programs you are to appear on, and the newspaper interviews you will have.

CHAPTER 4

THE MEDIA

TELEVISION—SEEING IS BELIEVING

Though still and infant industry, television is growing faster than any other medium. Never has there been such an effective and powerful channel of communication as TV. A television set can be found in nearly every home today.

In our society, where image building is a prerequisite to success, there is no better way than television to reach greater masses of people both quickly and efficiently.

Television is a demanding medium, having to satisfy both the eyes and ears simultaneously. It is seen and heard, producing a visual effect as well as verbal. Television captures a person's total attention.

Besides being able to convey a message verbally on TV, you also have the opportunity to show your message. On television, you can perform demonstrations, and bring visual aids and props to enhance and add color to your story or idea.

Not all television shows are alike. Each show varies in style and format, and appeals to selective groups of people. Most do not pay guests to appear, and the same holds true for, other media.

Television programs usually fall into one of three categories: variety/entertainment, news, and public affairs talk shows.

How To Create Your Own Publicity

There are shows seen nationally, produced either by networks or independent production companies. These shows are seen across the country. A few examples would be The Tonight Show, The Today Show and To Tell The Truth. Shows seen nationally benefit those guests interested in national publicity.

Local TV shows are generally more news and public affairs oriented, appealing to the local community. They come in a wide variety of shapes and forms. Some local shows will have a one-on-one interview. Some have several guests. A few have listener phone-ins, where viewers can call in, comment and/or ask questions of the guests being interviewed.

Try to arrive at your appointments on time. Allow yourself a few extra minutes, in the event that you get caught in traffic, or experience any other type of unexpected delay.

Dress neatly and avoid wearing jewelry. Wear colored clothes other than black and white. Check to see if the show has a make-up man, or if you're expected to do your own.

Always be relaxed when appearing on television. Your story will be more convincing. Never expect more than 10 or 15 minutes of on-air time. Know beforehand what you intend to say and talk about, so that you can make the best use of your time. Listen to the interviewer and pay special attention to what other guests are saying, so that you can comment and blend into the conversation. Never stare into the camera. Look at the interviewer. Look directly into the camera only if you wish to stress an important point to viewers. Don't try to hog a discussion. Be careful not to cut others off while they are talking. If your story is of a controversial subject, don't blow your cool if the interviewer, or someone else on the show, attacks your views. Showing maturity in situations like these gains support from viewers.

RADIO—IT'S ALL IN THE VOICE

Despite the power and prestige of television, radio continues to grow in size and popularity. Most families own at least one radio, and millions can be found in automobiles. We go to sleep with television, but wake up to radio.

Unlike television, with radio your only selling power is your voice. Your message is heard, but not seen. So, since people can't see you, your words must be able to make up for what can't be seen.

While television hooks you to the screen by imprisoning your eyes and ears, radio only captures your ears, and offers you freedom to pursue other interests while listening. Radio is a much less demanding medium. You can listen to radio while doing housework, or when driving in your car. Radio is the housewife's companion and the workingman's buddy to and from work.

Radio shows vary in format, as do TV programs. They also fall into the categories of variety/entertainment, news, and public affairs talk shows. There are radio programs heard nationally, but most are heard locally. Both AM and FM stations offer a wide variety of programming.

When interviewed on radio, speak in a pleasant and friendly tone. Talk normally without ever shouting. Speak clearly, in a language that listeners unfamiliar with your subject can understand.

NEWSPAPERS—EXTRA! EXTRA! READ ALL ABOUT IT!

People seeking publicity depend heavily on newspapers. Newspapers are the most widely used sources for local publicity, offering fast and dependable service.

One major advantage of receiving newspaper publicity is that when a story appears, the reader can put the paper down, and pick it up again later to refer back to or re-read a story. But on TV and radio, your message is delivered only once, and then it is gone.

There are three varieties of newspapers: local dailies; local weeklies; and nationals. Daily papers are usually printed five or six days each week, and can be morning, evening or afternoon editions. Local weeklies, as the name implies, are printed only once every week. National newspapers, like The National Enquirer and The Star, are generally printed once each week. Local papers emphasize community events and interests, whereas national papers prefer stories that have national appeal.

Two types of stories are found in newspapers—news and features. News stories are events of local or national importance. Feature stories are your human interest or off-beat stories. stories.

WIRE SERVICES—ONE CAN MAKE 100

Wire services are · also powerful outlets for attaining publicity. Wire services, like the Associated Press and United

Press International, sell their services (news and feature stories which come from places outside a local newspaper's domain), to newspapers all over the country. So, if your story is picked up by a wire service, it can run in hundreds of papers across the nation.

MAGAZINES—A TOUCH OF CLASS

Getting a story publicized in a magazine is a bit more difficult than in other media. More planning is involved, since stories must appeal to a national audience of readers.

Magazines are highly specialized, selective, and are sought after for the prestige they carry. Like newspapers, magazine stories have the advantage of being read, re-read, and passed along to family and friends. Magazines and newspapers offer this continued publicity.

A person will usually purchase a magazine because they are interested in a special market or theme which that magazine specializes in. When seeking magazine publicity, define your market, and seek out those publications which specialize in or have stories similar to yours. For example, if your story would appeal to single men, try Playboy. Or maybe you're promoting a flower shop? Then take a crack at Better Homes & Gardens.

When you seek national publicity, magazines, wire services and national newspapers are your best bets in the print media. In the electronic media, national TV and radio shows will do the trick. For extensive local publicity, stick to your local TV and radio shows and your local newspapers.

CHAPTER 5

PUBLICITY QUICKIES

THE PRESS RELEASE

So far we have been talking about long-term publicity campaigns, by first sending out a press kit and then reaching to grab tons of publicity on television, radio and in newspapers. But what about those of you not interested in planning an entire campaign and concerned only with learning how to get instant publicity in newspapers for a certain event such as a charity bazaar. For this coverage, you would merely write a press release.

The press release is submitted for publication to a newspaper for the sole purpose of promoting a timely event. Don't confuse this press release with the release described in Chapter 2, which is used in a major publicity campaign.

Some other examples of when you would use the press release are: engagement announcements, births, anniversaries, club meetings, exhibits, fund raising benefits, and election of officers. These are just a few of the many types of releases found in newspapers every day.

When writing a press release, certain ground rules must be followed. The press release must always be typed. Reporters and editors have little spare time to try and understand someone's handwriting, and to retype handwritten releases. A newspaper person will make any necessary corrections in pencil on your release, then submit it for printing. Always double-space your release so that there is sufficient space for the editor to make changes. Leave at least a one-inch margin on each side of the page. Your release should be limited to no more than a page or sometimes two.

Your release should be short, to the point, and not repetitious. Build your story into the shape of a pyramid by writing the most important point of the story at the beginning, and expanding to supporting points as you continue.

You must properly identify yourself by placing your name, address and telephone number at the top of the first page in the right-hand corner of the release. Type "FOR FURTHER INFORMATION CONTACT" above your name. If this information is not on the release the chances are most unlikely that your release will be printed. An editor may need to call you for additional information, and also, due to a responsibility to its readers, an editor won't print a story unless he's aware of the sources who supply him with the news. He must be certain that each story is valid.

After the heading, skip four lines and type in the release date, the date on which you want your story to appear. The release date is typed in capital letters and underlined. If you want your story to run immediately after being received by the newspaper, then type "FOR IMMEDIATE RELEASE." If you want the story to appear on a specific date, then type "FOR RELEASE ON MAY 7," or whatever your date may be.

If your story is to appear in a daily paper, I would suggest submitting the story at least one week before you want it to appear. If you're dealing with a weekly paper, submit your release about two weeks in advance. This will give the newspaper sufficient time to read the release, and prepare it for printing.

You can usually depend on a newspaper to print your release, especially your local or "hometown" paper which devotes most of its space to local matters. But don't wait until the last minute to submit your story, because it then might not be printed. Newspapers have limited space, and need time to plan in advance what stories will appear and when.

Next comes the dateline, four lines below the release date. The dateline, also typed in capital letters, tells the place (city) where the story occurred, or is going to take place. The dateline is typed at the beginning of the first paragraph, is followed by a dash, and then one space is skipped.

You're now ready to write the most important part of your release, the lead. The lead is the first paragraph of your story. The lead is usually just one sentence, and must tell the entire story in a nutshell. Think of it as if you were reading a newspaper. You scan the pages, looking at the printed stories. A headline captures your eye, you read the first paragraph, or lead, of that particular story, and if the story really evokes your interest, you will read on. Usually the first paragraph is enough to tell you what the story is about, and whether it interests you enough to read on. The lead tells the "meat," or main point of the story. See for yourself. Pick up a newspaper and try it.

Let's use as an example the following lead and analyze it;

Patrolman John Doe was voted "Policeman of the Year" at the annual policemen's dinner Tuesday night.

How To Create Your Own Publicity

A good lead will usually answer five very important questions. These questions are who, what, where, why and when. Let's see if the above example answers these questions. Firstly, who are we talking about? We are talking about John Doe. Next, what about John Doe? He was named policeman of the year. Where did this occur? It occurred at the annual policemen's dinner. Why did he receive this honor? Because he was voted most deserving. When did he receive this honor? He received this honor Tuesday night. So our lead sentence satisfies the five rules. It answers the questions of who, what, where, why and when.

After the lead is written, the remainder of the release should list important facts which support the lead, in order of importance. At the end of your story, type in either "-30-" or "###," which means the end. This tells the editor that your story is finished.

Pictures may also be sent to accompany your story, but may not always be printed because of lack of space. Examples of when pictures can be sent would be wedding and engagement announcements.

Don't be surprised or annoyed if an editor shortens or chops up your story. It happens every day. If a newspaper person feels that some of your story is unimportant, or that not enough space is available in the paper, he may delete much of what you have written until nothing but your lead remains. Again, you can see the importance of the lead. It must be able to stand alone.

Examples of the most common releases sent to newspapers for publication can be found on the following pages. These releases are relatively short and to the point. If you plan on writing a release similar to one of the examples, don't be afraid to add additional information if you feel that this information is important and pertinent to your story. But try to keep your release as short as possible.

SAMPLE RELEASE NO.1
WEDDING ANNOUNCEMENT

FOR FURTHER INFORMATION
CONTACT:
(Publicity Contact)
(Street Address)
(City, State, Zip Code)
(Telephone Number)

FOR IMMEDIATE RELEASE

ANYTOWN- In a double-ring ceremony in Anytown Church, on November 12, Linda Pepper and Frank David Smith were married. Rev. Andrew Phillips officiated at the ceremony. A reception followed at the Anytown Inn.

The bride is the daughter of Mr. and Mrs. Russell Pepper, 11-05 George St. The bridegroom is the son of Mrs. Smith of Newark.

Given in marriage by her father, the bride was attired in a white organza gown with venice lace outlining the V-neckline and bishop sleeves. The gown features a cathedral length veil with a matching headpiece.

Miss Ellen Fleming of Anytown, a friend of the bride, was Maid of Honor. Thomas Bush, friend of the groom, was Best Man.

Bridesmaids were Carol Lynch and Karen Sims, cousins of the bride.

The couple plans to reside in Anytown.

-30-

SAMPLE RELEASE NO.2
ENGAGEMENT

FOR FURTHER INFORMATION
CONTACT:
(Publicity Contact)
(Street Address)
(City, State, Zip Code)
(Telephone Number)

FOR IMMEDIATE RELEASE

ANYTOWN- Mr. and Mrs. John Doe, 11 State St., have announced the engagement of their daughter, Denise Emily, to Albert Henderson, son of Mr. and Mrs. Ralph Henderson, 5 Oak St.

A graduate of Anytown High School, Miss Doe is employed by the Anytown State Bank.

Her fiance was graduated from Empire High School, served with the Marine Corps for two years, and is currently employed by the Anytown Post Office.

No wedding date has yet been set.

-30-

SAMPLE RELEASE NO.3
WEDDING ANNIVERSARY

FOR FURTHER INFORMATION
CONTACT:
(Publicity Contact)
(Street Address)
(City, State, Zip Code)
(Telephone Number)

FOR IMMEDIATE RELEASE

ANYTOWN- Mr. and Mrs. John Doe celebrated their first wedding anniversary at a party recently at their home.

The couple was married January 6, 1975, at Anytown Church.

Mr. Doe is the son of Mr. and Mrs. Bill Doe of this community. Mrs. Doe is the daughter of Mr. and Mrs. Peter Lakes of Cherry Hill.

Mr. Doe is assistant manager at the Anytown Bakery.

-30-

SAMPLE RELEASE NO.4
BIRTH OF CHILD

FOR FURTHER INFORMATION
CONTACT:
(Publicity Contact)
(Street Address)
(City, State, Zip Code)
(Telephone Number)

FOR IMMEDIATE RELEASE

ANYTOWN- Mr. and Mrs. John Doe of this community announce the birth of their first child, a daughter, at Anytown Hospital at 10:01 a.m. on April 5.

The baby was named Amy, weighed five pounds at birth and measured 7 inches.

Mrs. Doe is the former Phyllis Smith of Miami, Fla.

Maternal grandparents are Mr. and Mrs. Joe Smith of Miami. Paternal grandparents are Mr. and Mr. Larry Doe of Anytown.

-30-

SAMPLE RELEASE NO.5   FOR FURTHER INFORMATION
CLUB MEETING   CONTACT:
                             (Publicity Contact)
                             (Street Address)
                             (City, State, Zip Code)
                             (Telephone Number)

FOR IMMEDIATE RELEASE

ANYTOWN- The Anytown Garden Club will hold a general meeting at the Women's Club, 20 State St., on September 11 at 10 a.m.

Louis and Jeannie Feliciano will speak on "Herb Gardening." Wayside herbs, as well as herbs for fragrance and drying are some of the subjects that will be covered.

Guests are welcome to attend.

-30-

SAMPLE RELEASE NO.6
CLUB EVENT

FOR FURTHER INFORMATION
CONTACT:
(Publicity Contact)
(Street Address)
(City, State, Zip Code)
(Telephone Number)

FOR RELEASE MAY 1

ANYTOWN- The Anytown Coin Club, sponsored by the Recreation Department, will hold its sixth annual Coin Show on Sunday, May 2, at the Anytown Athletic Club, on State St.

An exhibit of rare United States coins will be on display.

Hours for the show are 9 a.m. to 6 p.m. Admission is free.

-30-

SAMPLE RELEASE NO.7
PTA EVENT

FOR FURTHER INFORMATION
CONTACT:
(Publicity Contact)
(Street Address)
(City, State, Zip Code)
(Telephone Number)

FOR RELEASE FEBRUARY 28

ANYTOWN- The Anytown Senior High School Band Parents Association will hold a car wash today from 1:00 p.m. to 5:00 p.m. at the high school parking lot.

Last year's car wash was a big success. Bandmembers made $400, which paid for their trip to Wasington, D.C., to compete in the U.S. High School Band Contest. The band won a trophy for second place.

Now the group hopes to earn enough money to travel to Atlanta, Georgia, on June 24, where this year's competition will take place. This time bandmembers are shooting for the first place award.

-30-

SAMPLE RELEASE NO.8
FUND RAISER

FOR FURTHER INFORMATION
CONTACT:
(Publicity Contact)
(Street Address)
(City, State, Zip Code)
(Telephone Number)

FOR IMMEDIATE RELEASE

ANYTOWN- The Anytown High School PTA recently hosted a continental luncheon for the faculty at the school.

Youngsters from Anytown Elementary School provided the entertainment. The children read poems they had written about their teachers.

The PTA Executive Board prepared the lunch.

-30-

Publicity Quickies

SAMPLE RELEASE NO.9
GROUP TRIP

FOR FURTHER INFORMATION
CONTACT:
(Publicity Contact)
(Street Address)
(City, State, Zip Code)
(Telephone Number)

FOR IMMEDIATE RELEASE

ANYTOWN- Scouts of Troop 8 recently visited the Anytown National Park, spending two days camping by the ocean.

In addition to surf fishing and a guided tour of Ft. Hamilton and the old embattlements dating back to the late 1800's, the activities included investigating the Oak Lighthouse.

Scout Billy Doe, 8, won a box of cookies for finding the largest sea shell.

-30-

59

SAMPLE RELEASE NO. 10
GROUP TRIP PLANNED

FOR FURTHER INFORMATION
CONTACT:
(Publicity Contact)
(Street Address)
(City, State, Zip Code)
(Telephone Number)

FOR IMMEDIATE RELEASE

ANYTOWN- The Senior Citizens Club is planning a trip to the Anytown Museum on May 18, to be followed by an early dinner at the Clam House Restaurant.

Members are asked to send paid reservations (checks only) to John Doe, Senior Citizens Club chairman, Oak St. Checks should be made out to the Senior Citizens Club.

For further information call 788-9998.

-30-

SAMPLE RELEASE NO. 11
COMPANY PROMOTION

FOR FURTHER INFORMATION
CONTACT:
(Publicity Contact)
(Street Address)
(City, State, Zip Code)
(Telephone Number)

FOR IMMEDIATE RELEASE

ANYTOWN- Bruce Smith was named National Sales Manager of the Happy Department Store Co. on Saturday night at the company's annual executive dinner.

Mr. Smith had previously been District Sales Manager in the company's New York division.

In his new post, he is responsible for coordinating sales efforts for all company stores. He maintains his office in the chain's corporate headquarters in Anytown.

-30-

SAMPLE RELEASE NO. 12
ELECTION OF OFFICERS

FOR FURTHER INFORMATION
CONTACT:
(Publicity Contact)
(Street Address)
(City, State, Zip Code)
(Telephone Number)

FOR IMMEDIATE RELEASE

ANYTOWN- Mrs. Paula James was elected President of the Anytown Garden Club at the club's weekly luncheon Wednesday afternoon.

Mrs. James had served last year as Club Treasurer.

The luncheon was held at the Anytown Women's Club. Roast beef sandwiches were served, and entertainment was provided by the singing group, "The Melodies."

-30-

SAMPLE RELEASE NO. 13
COMMUNITY SERVICE
ANNOUNCEMENT

FOR FURTHER INFORMATION
CONTACT:
(Publicity Contact)
(Street Address)
(City, State, Zip Code)
(Telephone Number)

FOR IMMEDIATE RELEASE

ANYTOWN- The police department will give free blood pressure readings from 10 a.m. to 4 p.m., Saturday, at police headquarters.

Two nurses will assist Dr. Joseph McDonald in taking the readings. Those interested in having their blood pressure read may call Police Chief Ronald Summer at 788-9994.

"The reason for this program is to refer people with high blood pressure to a physician," Summer said.

-30-

FOLLOW-UP STORIES

If you had a release printed in the paper which publicized an upcoming event, you can write a follow-up story describing how the event turned out. This is another way to get additional publicity for yourself or your group.

Let's use release number 8 as our example, the fund raising car wash for the high school band. After the car wash, if bandmembers earn enough money to pay for their trip, another release could be written stating that fact. Still another release could be written prior to the group's trip to Atlanta, and another when the group returns after the competition telling how they fared.

A NEWSPAPER "LETTER TO THE EDITOR"

Another way of speaking your mind and obtaining free publicity is by writing a letter to the Editor. Most newspapers encourage their readers to write these letters. A letter to the Editor is a letter sent to a newspaper, to the editor's attention. It pertains to a specific problem or point of view a reader might have.

A letter to the Editor is printed exactly as it is received from the reader. A letter to the Editor is the perfect outlet for voicing your opinion on issues, and for making your neighbors aware of the problem situation. This is how the teacher, disgusted with deplorable conditions within the school system, can speak his piece. So can the housewife, angered by a stop sign on her street which was knocked down and never replaced.

Letters to the Editor are powerful weapons which produce

public awareness, thus influencing change and betterment within a community. These letters get action because they are read by most readers (housewives, businessmen, politicians, policemen) who are interested or influenced by what their neighbors are thinking.

To write a letter to the Editor, simply address your letter to Editor, followed by the name and address of the newspaper. Always sign your letter and write the city where you reside underneath your name.

COLUMN ITEMS

If you look through your newspaper, you'll notice weekly columns devoted to specific topics like sports, society, entertainment, politics, business, medicine, education, and the like. When you think that your story idea would be suitable for mention in a certain column, contact the writer of that column.

TV AND RADIO SERVICE ANNOUNCEMENTS

The Federal Communications Commission (FCC), the federal agency which licenses and regulates all TV and radio stations, requires that these stations allot a reasonable amount of time for public service programming and announcements.

For those of you wishing to publicize a public service message, e.g., rent controlled housing for the elderly, free time is often available. Usually your release or message is broadcast over the air by station personnel. Sometimes you might even be invited to appear on television or radio to present the announcement yourself.

Your public service release should be prepared the same as if you were writing a press release. The same rules govern. The public service release must be short, usually not exceeding a paragraph or two. Also, the time it takes to read the release and the amount of words in it must be listed.

If your or your group desire air time contact the Community Affairs Director or Program Manager at the station you wish to be on.

An example of a TV/radio public service release can be studied on the following page.

SAMPLE PUBLIC SERVICE
RELEASE FOR TV AND RADIO

FOR FURTHER INFORMATION
CONTACT:
(Publicity Contact)
(Street Address)
(City, State, Zip Code)
(Telephone Number)

FOR IMMEDIATE RELEASE

TIME-12 seconds
WORDS- 29

ANYTOWN- The Anytown Orphan Society is seeking families who can provide a loving home to orphaned children.

If you wish to adopt a child, please call Mrs. Doe at 088-4152.

-30-

TV AND RADIO EDITORIALS

To satisfy FCC regulations, and to provide a service to their listeners, TV and radio stations often air editorials. On an editorial, a station representative will present opinions on controversial issues which reflect the views of the management of that station. Responsible spokesmen with contrasting views are offered on the air rebuttal time to give their side of the issue or issues. This is another fine opportunity for you to speak your mind and receive publicity.

PUBLICITY STUNTS

There are a million and one publicity stunts used every day by clever publicists. If you think hard, you can probably come up with a few of your own.

Publicity stunts get instant and overwhelming attention if properly planned.

Marches, parades and demonstrations are some of the most common and successful publicity stunts used.

If a group of residents are disgusted with porno movies playing in their neighborhood, they can plan and stage a protest demonstration in front of the theatre playing the movies. Guaranteed, the media will cover this event. Chances are, by later that night, protesters will see themselves on TV, hear about themselves on radio, and read about themselves in the newspaper.

Another example of a publicity stunt would be for the company who made the porno movie to plan a protest in front of the theatre. They could use their own people to picket the theatre and to carry protest signs. They probably wouldn't be hurting themselves, because the publicity received would only inspire more people into wanting to see the movie because of its controversy.

BULLETIN BOARDS

To get added publicity, list all your announcements and events on paper or posters, and put them on display in stores, schools, churches, anywhere where they will be read by the people you are trying to reach.

CABLE TV

Cable TV is a relatively new but growing industry whose shows usually cater to select interest groups. If your community has Cable TV, check out the programs aired to see if a guest appearance would be to your benefit.

CHAPTER 6

LEARNING THE SHOWS

I've already described to you the various types of television and radio shows, and newspapers and magazines whose doors are open for free publicity. Now we can take a look at a sampling of each on the following pages.

You will find examples of the following shows and publications: a national network television show; a nationally syndicated television show; a local public affairs television show; a local television news show; a local television variety show; a national radio news show; a local variety radio show; a local public affairs radio show; a national weekly newspaper; a local daily newspaper; a local weekly newspaper; and a national magazine.

Familiarize yourself with the formats of each show and publication.

Penny Price: Talent Coordinator

GOOD MORNING AMERICA
ABC-TV, NEW YORK
PENNY PRICE: TALENT COORDINATOR
(EXAMPLE OF A NATIONAL NETWORK TV SHOW)

Actor David Hartman is the host of this popular early morning show. *Good Morning America* is seen live, Monday through Friday, from 7:00 a.m. to 9:00 a.m., by millions of viewers across the country. Other contributing personalities on the show are Geraldo Rivera, former New York City Mayor John Lindsay, and Ms. Hollywood herself, the witty Rona Barrett.

The program combines the elements of news, controversy and on-location features, in a magazine-type format.

Penny Price, a former talent coordinator on the Mike Douglas Show, calls *Good Morning America* a people program. She looks for energetic personalities behind guests and stories.

72

Mimi O'Brien, Associate Producer on television's To Tell The Truth Show, goes to all ends of the earth looking for guests. Will the real Mimi O'Brien please stand up?

TO TELL THE TRUTH
PRODUCED BY GOODSON-TODMAN ENTERPRISES, LTD.
MIMI O'BRIEN: ASSOCIATE PRODUCER
(EXAMPLE OF A NATIONALLY SYNDICATED TV SHOW)

TO TELL THE TRUTH is an entertaining half-hour quiz show, hosted by television and radio personality Gary Moore.

One central character with an unusual story or background, plus two other people acting as imposters, are selected in an effort to stump four celebrity panelists. Panelists, by asking questions, must decide which of the three is for real and which are the imposters.

It's a fun show and viewers can play along at home. The show is seen on about 100 stations throughout the United States, and is most popular with people over 40 and school children. Being a nationally syndicated show, *TO TELL THE TRUTH* offers a guest national exposure, the best form of publicity going.

73

Gwen Barrett, Associate Producer of WNEW-TV's Midday Live Show, is in outer space surrounded by Stars.

THE MIDDAY LIVE SHOW
WNEW-TV, METROMEDIA
NEW YORK, CHANNEL 5
GWEN BARRETT: ASSOCIATE PRODUCER
(EXAMPLE OF A LOCAL PUBLIC AFFAIRS TV SHOW)

This local public affairs show is on live, Monday through Friday, from 1:00 p.m. to 2:30 p.m. It's one of New York's most popular talk shows.

Hosted by Bill Boggs, a viewer will find a wide array of guests and discussions. Well-known people in a variety of fields, civic leaders, and local residents appear to speak on issues of interest and importance to the community, nation and world.

The show addresses itself to serious topics and the arts, and attracts all types of people, especially those interested in the complex social problems we face today. A debate on a timely controversial issue is part of every day's show.

74

Alec Nagle takes a breather after WABC-TV's Eyewitness News Show.

6 O'CLOCK EYEWITNESS NEWS
WABC-TV, NEW YORK
CHANNEL 7
ALEC NAGLE: PRODUCER
(EXAMPLE OF A LOCAL TV NEWS SHOW)

EYEWITNESS NEWS exemplifies your local news show, catering to women in the 18 to 49 age bracket. This show boasts top-notch reporter Geraldo Rivera.

It was the first news show to develop the individual personalities of its reporters. When you watch the show you get the feeling that the reporters are all pals, are as human as the next guy, and that the *EYEWITNESS NEWS* studio is a relaxed and fun place to be. In fact, this format proved so successful that other news shows began copying the idea.

Much air-time is devoted to human interest features, self-help stories and what Alec Nagle calls fun stories.

Joe Franklin waits for his director's cue before opening a show.

THE JOE FRANKLIN SHOW
WOR-TV, NEW YORK
CHANNEL 9
JOE FRANKLIN: HOST
(EXAMPLE OF A LOCAL TV VARIETY SHOW)

This show is hosted by one of the best liked men in the business. Joe Franklin started many of today's stars on the road to fame.

The show is taped, and aired the following day, once in the morning and a second time late at night.

Nicknamed the "King of Nostalgia," Joe chats with interesting and knowledgeable guests from all walks of life. Whether it be Liza Minnelli, or John, the neighborhood butcher, they all feel right at home on Joe's show.

Lannie Spalding takes a cigarette break between interviews on NBC.

NEWS AND INFORMATION SERVICE (NIS)
NBC RADIO, ALL-NEWS
LANNIE SPALDING: WRITER & TALENT COORDINATOR
(EXAMPLE OF NATIONAL ALL-NEWS RADIO FORMAT)

NBC NEWS AND INFORMATION SERVICE feeds over 80 all-news stations across the nation, seven days a week, 24 hours a day.

Besides covering national and world news, feature stories in a variety of categories are also aired. Interesting people and authorities from various fields are interviewed. Topics ranging from human interest, consumer interest, health and science reports, to travel and entertainment are covered.

Like most all-news formats, the audience is generally middle-aged business people. Lannie Spalding says that *NIS* is now also capturing a larger percentage of the 18 to 30-year-old group.

77

Arlene Francis and her producer, Jean Bach, chat in the studio before going on the air.

THE ARLENE FRANCIS SHOW
WOR-RADIO, NEW YORK
JEAN BACH: PRODUCER
(EXAMPLE OF LOCAL RADIO VARIETY TALK SHOW)

Arlene Francis, talented TV and radio star, is hostess for this interview talk show. She was a regular on the *What's My Line* television show.

Arlene's show attracts people from all walks of life, and is one of New York's most popular and highly rated radio shows.

The program is on Monday through Friday from 10:15 a.m. to 11:00 a.m. WOR-Radio has one of the strongest radio signals in the country, and captures the largest audiences. Producer Jean Bach says she tries to cater to everyone.

78

Amy Goldberg is all smiles, as she keeps her eyes open for a good story on WCBS-FM.

CHANGES
WCBS-FM RADIO, NEW YORK
AMY GOLDBERG: DIRECTOR, PUBLIC AFFAIRS
(EXAMPLE OF LOCAL PUBLIC AFFAIRS RADIO SHOW)

Because of the music format, ''Oldies but Goodies,'' this show's audience is primarily the 18 to 35-year-old group.

To satisfy FCC requirements for public affairs programming, program personnel spend much of their time going out into the community, setting up meetings and luncheons, to find out what people are thinking about, and what their problems are.

After this research is completed, they select a series of problem topics to cover, notify the FCC of these topics, and report on them. Thus, answering the public's need for community affairs programming is the job of Amy Goldberg.

Peter Faris is pleased. He's just made a big scoop on a great story for The Star.

THE STAR

PETE FARIS: EDITOR

(EXAMPLE OF NATIONAL WEEKLY NEWSPAPER)

THE STAR appeals to a very broad, middle-class readership. Normally, the purchaser is a female supermarket shopper, from age 25 to 65, much the same as the National Enquirer's audience.

Pete Faris describes the paper as colorful and accurately informative. Time and Newsweek have described *THE STAR* as a racey tabloid.

The paper seeks interesting stories of people from all socio-economic groups, and being a national paper, stories must appeal to a national audience. About four million people read the paper each week! That's what you call popularity.

*What's up John Koster? He looks like he knows something that we don't.
I guess we'll just have to wait and read about it in tomorrow's Bergen
Record.*

THE BERGEN RECORD
HACKENSACK, NEW JERSEY
JOHN KOSTER: MUNICIPAL REPORTER
(EXAMPLE OF A DAILY-LOCAL NEWSPAPER)

THE RECORD is committed to cover the 70 towns of Bergen County,
New Jersey, so that people will know what's going on in their individual
towns, as well as the rest of the county, state, nation and world, in order of
diminishing importance for the paper.

The paper focuses primarily on county and state news. The record has a
weekly readership of about 150,000, and a weekend circulation of 200,000.

John Koster, municipal reporter and nationally known author and
lecturer, describes his audience as a very heterogeneous group. Bergen
County is an area that ranges from people in the upper income brackets, to
those persons living on welfare and social security. John says that the bulk of
readership would be middle-class, somewhat above the national average in
income and education.

81

Jane Salek, Editor: The Shopper, Fairlawn, N.J.

THE SHOPPER
FAIR LAWN, NEW JERSEY
JANE SALEK: EDITOR
(EXAMPLE OF A WEEKLY-LOCAL NEWSPAPER)

THE SHOPPER, delivered free of charge, is a local, family oriented paper. The paper emphasizes local news and events of interest to community members.

Clubs, religious organizations, and school groups, to name but a few, find the local-weekly paper their best friend when it comes to publicity. People read these papers to find out what's going on in their town and immediate areas.

The paper covers a nine-town area with a 64,000 circulation. There are also two weekend editions, called the News-Beacon and Dispatch, which cover a three-town area. These are paid weeklies, and are more heavily oriented to municipal news.

Hal Wingo is tired after a hard day's work. But he's never too tired to learn about an interesting person for People Magazine.

PEOPLE MAGAZINE
PUBLISHED BY TIME, INC.
HAL WINGO: SENIOR NEWS EDITOR
(EXAMPLE OF A NATIONAL MAGAZINE)

PEOPLE MAGAZINE is one of America's leading success stories. Almost overnight, the magazine has grown to become one of America's favorite publications. When Dinah Shore devotes an entire show to honoring *PEOPLE MAGAZINE,* you can't help but take notice. *PEOPLE* is a lively pictorial magazine devoted to all types of interesting persons, and individuals in the news, who are in and out of the spotlight..

With a circulation over two million, *PEOPLE* readers are a relatively young group, ranging in age from 18 to 38. More than 60% of the readers are college educated people who are interested in what's happening in all fields, from show business to religion.

Hal Wingo says his readers are an aware group, people who have curiousity and interest in other human beings, and want to know more about them.

83

CHAPTER 7

MEETING THE PROS

Now that you've read about their shows and publications, it's time to introduce you to some of today's most prominent and influential media people. Read and compare their answers to a series of questions I have asked them on what makes a good guest or story. I selected specific questions that I feel you, the reader, would ask.

Get to know these people. They are the ones responsible for selecting guests, stories, and ideas for the shows and publications described in Chapter 6. And they are typical of the people you will be dealing with directly on your own.

Read about what it takes to get on a national TV show, and how the requirements differ greatly from a local TV show. What type of person does the radio producer want you to be prior to putting you on her show? Are you fit for print in a newspaper? Are you interesting enough to be in a magazine?

How to Create Your Own Publicity

QUESTION 1

WHAT TYPES OF PEOPLE AND STORIES DO YOU LOOK FOR?

Penny Price, ABC-TV, *Good Morning America*- Guests that will fit into our magazine format. With our magazine format that covers just about everybody. We really want the show to be a people show. We try to get into the personalities of all our guests, and have lively, interesting, feature stories. We look for the human interest and newsbreaker stories.

Mimi O'Brien, Goodson-Todman Enterprises, Ltd. *To Tell The Truth*- All kinds. Especially the first-of-a-kind types.

Gwen Barrett, WNEW-TV, Metromedia, *Midday Live*- We run the gamut. We look for interesting people that you would not ordinarily find on other shows, or read about. For example, we have had on, from time to time, people who have advertised for mates in various newspapers. Well, one day we read an ad by this woman who was looking for a husband who possessed Adonis qualities. The guy had to be handsome, be a certain height, make a certain income, etc., etc. Anyway, we became curious and invited her on the program. You wouldn't believe this woman. She looked like a fish. P.S., we didn't find her a husband.

Alec Nagle, WABC-TV, *Eyewitness News*- Besides the basic news stories, people stories. Those stories which people can really relate to. Like the old lady is being evicted. And the more visual the story, the better chance of it getting on the air.

Joe Franklin, WOR-TV, *Joe Franklin Show*- I'll take all kinds. I'll do two or three big names, like today I have Lynn Redgrave and Tony Martin, and then I'll also put on the photographer who wants to plug her exhibition, or the sculptor who's plugging his exhibition. A lot of people say I'm a nice guy because I never turn anyone down. I try to be a nice guy, and to help people but I do turn down. For everyone you see on my show there are 1,000 more that I don't have time to put on. But I turn these people down in a gracious way.

Lannie Spalding, NBC-Radio, *News and Information Service*- The people down on the news desk cover the day-breaking stories and hard news items. Here, we are concerned about features, features which must generally satisfy national audiences. But sometimes we can take a local story and make it of national interest. A good example would be a Broadway show which could never sustain itself solely on a New York audience. So we get news out about a good Broadway show, and when the family from Ohio comes to town, they're going to see that show. Here we are responsible for features on entertainment, the arts, and that covers almost anything.

Jean Bach, WOR-Radio, *Arlene Francis Show*- Stories that have some relationship to the listener, either from the standpoint of curiousity or personal involvement. A program on how I danced with the President would spark curiousity and interest. A program on how to save money is obviously of great value to everyone.

Amy Goldberg, WCBS-Radio, *Changes*- News oriented stories. But again, it might be summer, and so people are gardening, or maybe interested in what they are going to do with their kids for the summer, or wondering where to go on vacation. Now this isn't really public affairs, so you try to work out an angle to turn these topics into public affairs presentations. I also look for plain, interesting people to talk with. If you can get someone interesting to sit and talk with, he might just have something interesting to say. A lot of people are interested in listening to interesting people, people from their community who are not necessarily celebrities.

87

How to Create Your Own Publicity

Pete Faris, *The Star*- We look for ordinary people, and are always interested in celebrities, because people are always interested in what their favorite movie star is doing. For example, Americans almost have a natural fascination with the Kennedys. And the Kennedy family sells for us. We also go for the ordinary Joe. If you look through our paper you'll see ordinary people, who are doing extraordinary things. And another thing. We are a national newspaper, and have to appeal to a national audience, but there are stories that don't have to be national to appeal to people. It can be the story of the little old pig farmer from up in Des Moines, Iowa. This story, if unusual or human interest, can have appeal to everyone. We look for human interest in its broadest sense. You also have health. People are fascinated by their bodies and what goes wrong with them. So whenever we see a good medical story, maybe a new technique on heart disease or the latest thing in kidney transplants, we'll do them. People love to be given answers to their problems. We also try to keep our stories as factual as possible, and not like fan magazines, like I was raped by a female werewolf.

John Koster, *Bergen Record*- When you're dealing with ordinary middle-class people you have to remember that as vital as their lives are to the welfare of the nation, as a rule, they're not terribly interesting. When we cover events that are not necessarily hard news, like politics, murder, fires, we look for stuff that's colorful. One indication of whether something would make a good story is, would it make a good picture? So if it's a good picture possibility, there's always a better chance of us using the story. Let's say a group is having a fund raising affair. If they can get some of their members to dress up in costumes, it would be a very good angle. This would probably get them a picture and story in the paper. Let's face it, everyone wants publicity, and if you want it badly enough you have to think up a good angle.

Jane Salek, *The Shopper*- We look for a lot of human interest with a local angle.

Meeting The Pros

Hal Wingo, *People Magazine*- The only angle each story has to have is a personality focus. There is hardly any story that can't be told in that way. We look for a person who is the focal point of a situation or event, or who has had a personal experience in their life which makes them interesting. These people can be anybody, from the top stars to our next door neighbors. Big names appear on our covers, but once you get inside the magazine, it touches on every area. You don't have to be famous to get into *People*.

QUESTION 2
WHERE AND HOW DO YOU FIND YOUR
GUESTS OR INTERVIEWEES? DO YOU
SEEK THEM OUT OR DO THEY COME TO YOU?

Price- We think about our audience. And we just don't want to have the same people that are on all the other shows. So usually we go out and find our own interesting people. But that doesn't mean we won't take a good and interesting guest who is offered to us.

O'Brien- We have talent coordinators who read all the newspapers and magazines and select guests and stories for possible use. We then sit down and discuss which stories we would like to use. Also, people call and write to us with their ideas. How about you, Steve? Are you handling any interesting people now?

Barrett- It's an equal combination of both.

Nagle- The assignment desk gets them in phone calls. People call with tips, or with something they would like to do. And we get them from wire services and newspapers. When we get a serious tip, or really good story idea, we'll send out a reporter to check it out.

Franklin- I've never called a guest in my life. I'm embarrassed because a show like mine is local and doesn't pay guests. I figure that word gets around about me. It goes back already 15 years when I was in radio, where Cary Grant would come to town, and he would say that Tony Curtis told him to come on my show. Usually, whenever a big name comes to town they ask to do my show, and so does everyone else looking for publicity.

Spalding- Each of us working here has a certain expertise in different fields, so we do have our contacts. And then people call us...public relations firms, and individuals who have ideas and guests. Besides, we are national, and can generally get who we want. John Erlichman was in today and did an hour.

Bach- It's about 50-50. We know in advance what public figures are coming to town, and then people also call us.

Goldberg- Both. As you know there are a lot of public relations outfits in this city, and there a lot of people out promoting themselves. That's good, because there are many times when you really rely on that. Also, I get four or five newspapers a day, plus all the leading magazines. You have to go through all these publications, because they give you program ideas.

Faris- We get many story ideas, and if a story seems worthwhile, I'll follow it up. Based on that follow up, we'll decide whether we'll go ahead and really get into it, or merely drop the story.

Koster- Both. Garden clubs, political groups, churches, and whatever have you groups, send us press releases announcing events and meetings. Besides printing these releases, the reporters check further into them, to find out if one of these events would be worth a larger feature story or a photograph. Every once in a while you come across something that would.

Salek- I would say the answer is both. We are always flooded with releases people send into us. We also do some digging on our own.

Wingo- We have a network of correspondents around the world working for us full and part-time. They suggest a lot of material we use, especially when it comes to finding the unknowns. Sometimes we know certain people we would like to do stories on, and agressively go after them, and then publicity people suggest story ideas to us.

ARE THERE CERTAIN TOPICS, STORY IDEAS OR PEOPLE THAT
YOU TEND TO STAY AWAY FROM, OR THAT AUTOMATICALLY
TURN YOU OFF?

Price- I would never book anyone coming to town who is just interested in
promoting something, and that's all they want to talk about. The person
would also have to have other interesting things about him, because
again, we want to make the show a people program. When I worked on
the Mike Douglas Show, we made the show work, because we made it
interesting and different from others. Let's say we had an author on,
and we learned that he was interested in baseball. Well, then we did
baseball with him. The author got publicity for his book, and we got an
interesting guest. So we really dug into things and did our homework.
The show was always alive. It's the same thing here. We really want to
make people look different than they would on any other show. We
want to get into their personalities and make them come alive.

O'Brien- Not unless the idea is tasteless, offensive, or too controversial.
And since we are syndicated, a show might not run until six or eight weeks
after taping, so we tend to stay away from certain news stories where
new developments might occur prior to airing the show.

Barrett- No, with an explanation. Many times people turn us off, but many
times we'll book these people despite the fact that we find them
extremely obnoxious. And we'll do what we call...set them up. By this
I mean we'll bring them on with someone equally as talented. It's true.
We'll do this when it comes to a controversial issue, or a subject we feel
our viewers would be interested in.

Nagle- Personally, I'm not wild, for some reason, about old people stories.
And I'm not wild about politicians. The majority of our viewers are,
though. I'm not wild about talking heads either, meaning film with just

a person in front of a camera talking. This is one of the lowest forms of journalism. If we do cover a story, we like visuals or action behind the person, to illustrate what that person is talking about. This will usually improve the story.

Franklin- I'd go along with anything today, but I'd rather stay away from what I'm hearing so much about lately. It seems every third program I see now, I'm hearing something about premature ejaculation, and orgasms, orgasms, and more orgasms. I think subjects like these are best read. I think it goes too fast on TV to be properly covered.

Spalding- The only time we usually stay away from somebody is when that person is overexposed, a person who did the Johnny Carson show and every other show. And there are things that turn us off...the people who are too selfish in their interests and reasons for publicity. We don't do commercials, we do interesting stories.

Bach- Very in depth stories about sports, with long detailed lists of scores are of no interest to our audience, or they would be listening to one of those shows. We stay away from anything which is highly technical. If we did do a show, let's say with a sport's figure, we would not go into batting averages. The interview would be more of a personal nature. How does he feel competing against someone else? We try to pull out the human quality in each guest.

Goldberg- I have to stay away, by definition, from certain shows and ideas that don't fall into the public affairs category. And there are other topics, one would be the women's movement, that are old stories. There are a lot of books and material still being written, but there's nothing really new in the movement. We've heard it all. There are so many books on this subject, and they seem to always come in cycles. I start to really turn away from the women's movement and other topics, unless someone gives me something new. I try to stay away from topics that have been overdone. It's the same thing with the psychological self-help books.

How to Create Your Own Publicity

Faris- Yes, anything that's down. Every story we do in the Star, we like to leave our readers feeling up at the end. We might make them cry while reading the story, but it will have a happy ending. It's like the pot of gold at the end of the rainbow. Anything that is down, down, down all the way, we tend to stay away from. But that doesn't stop us from taking a serious look at mentally retarded people from time to time, or handicapped people, because these topics are a reality. If a handicapped person has succeeded at something, or has overcome a major obstacle, it makes for an interesting story.

Koster- You tend to stay away from doing features on anything that's highly political, or anything that's going to present only one point of view. Usually, you stay away from people who are too agressive and demanding, and tell you that you have to do something, or it was done this way in the past.

Salek- Not really, unless it's something distasteful.

Wingo- No, we have never made any decision that we wouldn't touch any one specific personality or story.

WHAT TYPES OF STORIES SEEM TO SPARK THE MOST INTEREST WITH YOUR LISTENERS OR READERS?

Price- Anything that's in the news or is newsworthy, because we're a news entertainment program. And during the first hour of the show, anything that's of interest to men who are listening before going to work. Like sports. Men are at home the first hour. And the second hour we cater to housewives. Anything to do with kids, health, beauty, and anything else women would regard as interesting.

O'Brien- Stories about how someone can look younger. We get more fan mail on this than on any other subject.

Barrett- Definitely the controversial issues.

Nagle- Major news stories, like a plane crash. Also, appeals from members of the community. Someone's in need of help, or in serious trouble. And service stories...like how to repair a lamp. Human interest and self-help stories spark the greatest response from viewers.

Franklin- On my show it's the famous entertainers.

Spalding- Health. Put on a story about a new drug, diet or nutrition, and you get mail like crazy. We don't get much mail on the esoteric issues of the day, but a person will write in wanting to know more about the drug that Dr. Frank Field was talking about.

Bach- Recently, we got tons of phone calls and letters because we did a program on the religious cults. I was very amazed that we didn't get more negative flack. It was mostly people saying that these things have to be brought to light. These were parents who lost their children to the Moon cult and other groups. It was terribly touching, and everybody's

95

interested in it. It's a phenomenon that's current in New York. Also, people always respond to personal trouble...drunkenness, or anything that has a personal problem factor. We were the first show to do a program on breast cancer, and that got a tremendous response. Programs that deal with human problems stay with the listeners.

Goldberg- Anything which gives the public an instant answer. People want to be able to say, "what does it mean that I did this?," be it a dream or whatever. People love any kind of guidance, and you get an immediate response. People want easy answers all the time, and that's why all the self-help books sell like mad. So maybe I'm contradicting myself by not giving this to my listeners. But many of these topics, I feel as a producer, do not serve the public interest and are not worth promoting.

Faris- Health and how-to's. Like how to make yourself more glamorous looking and sexy, or how to get a better job. Anything that can help better one's life or make it more enjoyable. Anything that involves the consumer. We do stories on medical breakthroughs, UFO's on occasion, ghosts and other things that go bump in the night. People have a fascination for these sorts of things, but we keep them on the light side.

Koster- Anything that has to do with animals or children. I remember one kid found this oversized snapping turtle that weighed over 100 pounds. We put in the story that this kid was going to make it into soup. We got phone calls, we got letters, we got protests, we got threats of legal action. Finally, the kid was forced to take the turtle out and turn it loose, instead of cooking soup. Then there was a story about a female dog and her puppies that were found in the basement of a burned-out house. The reporter opened the lead of the story by saying, female dog named Fluffy and her puppies will die in the ASPCA's gas chambers unless someone calls to adopt them within 24 hours. Well, within 24 hours we had so many phone calls, that they were not only able to give away Fluffy and all her pups, but they were also able to clean out the pound. For once, every animal in that shelter was adopted. People really turn on to human interest stuff.

96

Meeting The Pros

Salek- Stories that issue an appeal for something are the ones that evoke tremendous response. We ran a story about a 17-year-old boy who needed open heart surgery, but his parents couldn't afford to send him to California for the needed operation. It was not such a spectacular story, but the response was tremendous. We received letters at this office with money in them. We have run stories from time to time about little kids who need parenting, or somebody needs blood. Surprisingly enough, in this day and age, if it's a hard luck story, it gets a lot of response.

Wingo- The best known faces in America today are faces from television. And the people who have sold best for us are personalities from television. Our recent cover story on Henry Winkler, The Fonz, from ABC-TV's Happy Days, was an absolute blockbuster. Other times when we do stories on people who are different or controversial, we get tremendous response.

WHAT TYPE OF PUBLICITY PERSON SUCCEEDS WITH YOU THE MOST? WHAT TYPE FAILS THE MOST?

Price-The person who knows the show, and knows what I need and look for. The person who understands my needs will be the most successful. And I love people to be as creative as possible, to not only suggest guests and ideas, but also help me plan a segment. It helps if they get film pieces, props, a relative of the guest, anything that would make the story more human and interesting.

O'Brien-The low-key person, who isn't pushy. The person who not only tells you the good points of a story, but also the bad. For example, the woman really isn't as pretty as she appears to be in the picture. So above all, be honest.

Barrett-The ones that take me out for lobster lunches, like you, Steve. No, seriously, we're only human, and we find that we are more responsive to the publicity person with whom we've established a rapport. Give us a good story or guest once, and we'll be even more cooperative the next time, because we know we can trust the person. But unfortunately, if you make a mistake once, it's very, very hard to try to correct it. So if you give us a guest who doesn't live up to our expectations, or your promises, you'll find yourself in trouble the next time.

Nagle-People who understand that stories must be set up, be visual, that all that they want to get across possibly isn't what we want gotten across. People who let us play our game with it also, and who don't try to set up a story as totally theirs, are helpful.

Franklin-The publicity person who fails has a need to fail...they have a need to be turned down. Many people are on ego trips, and know in their hearts they don't merit being on a major talk show. These are the people

98

who have nothing to say or promote, but just need attention. The ones that succeed the most with me are people who help me organize or package a theme for my show. They'll call up and say I'm an actress who is now an artist, and I will bring along three other people who are ex-actors, or actresses who have switched into that so-called double occupational society. Now I have a theme. This would help anyone get on my show, to help me organize the show. It helps me out a lot when a person seeking publicity can suggest a theme or topic.

Spalding-I can't stand a hard sell person. I like someone who is matter of fact when they call. The person who deals honestly in a businesslike way. I won't tolerate someone trying to cram something down my throat. Or those persons who tell me I'm making a big mistake when I give them a no on a guest. I'm much more receptive to the person with whom I've dealt with before. And if this person calls with another idea I'm really not crazy about, I might still do it because I've developed a trust and rapport with this person. Trust is important.

Bach-If someone double-crosses us, that's just rotten. Especially when we're promised a guest, and that guest doesn't show. We understand the human error, because even here we're doing 50 things at once. But be honest with us, and be considerate.

Goldberg-I wanted to do a program on the singles scene in New York City, and a man called me up and said he was involved with an organization where you sign up and get a membership to this single's group. It sounded interesting, and he made many suggestions, and was very helpful. It sounded interesting until he went too far. I felt everything he was doing was merely to promote his own organization. He gave me the name of this person and that person, and told me to do this and that. I don't know. It turned me off to hear one man have all the answers. I can't stand it when a person tries to push something down my throat.

Faris- The publicity person who succeeds is the one who guarantees me a good story on an exclusive basis. Let's take an example using a celebrity.

Robert Redford is classified as usually unattainable for an interview. But we arranged to do a major piece on Redford, and got him to talk about his homelife...the money he makes. We spent about three hours talking to him on a plane. This is the greatest of examples, but anyone who suggests a good or unusual story can succeed with us.

Koster-The people who succeed the most, are the most frank and honest about what they really have. A person who is forceful, without being too agressive. If you really want to be successful, have an interesting story, and think pictorially.

Salek-The type that gives me clean copy succeeds the most. When someone sends me a release or announcement it should be neat and clean.

Wingo- People who understand our magazine succeed the best with us. The ones that try to push stories or subjects on us without any real understanding of what we are trying to do, are the ones who fail consistently. We appreciate the role of publicists when they bring us information that's useful to us. We work very closely with these people, and they are very helpful to us in the production of the magazine. And people who can't take no for an answer fail all the time, too.

QUESTION 6

WHAT ADVICE WOULD YOU OFFER THE PERSON SEEKING PUBLICITY FOR THE FIRST TIME?

Price-I'd say don't be scared, and get your ideas together before you call. Most importantly, know when the guest is available to do the show, because I book my guests by the week. And be prepared to have a pre-show interview. I never put a guest on the show who I haven't pre-interviewed in person.

O'Brien-This person must be short, to the point, knowledgeable on their subject. And when sending information, be specific and brief.

Barrett- Know your subject, and prepare an impressive press kit.

Nagle-Call us if you have an interesting or newsworthy item. Be able to express what it is you wish to accomplish. We like to do fun stories...our show is based on the personalities of our reporters. Call in the story. Get as much of the ground preparation done as possible, so we don't have to do it on the phone. Tell us who the story is about, and what it is about.

Franklin-Above all, be honest and don't con. Don't talk fast and most importantly, be familiar with the show. There's nothing that puts down a talk show host or talent coordinator more than somebody who just thinks of you as merchandise. They want on the air publicity, and they've never even seen your show. This happens to me every once in a while, and that is the ultimate put down. Someone will call up and say I'd like to be a guest on your show, and I'll say, in a devious route, do you think you'll fit in and blend with the flavor and rhythm of my panel? The person will say I don't know...I've never seen your show. That's just a terrible insult.

101

How to Create Your Own Publicity

Spalding-I would want a call on the phone...a nice friendly call...a preliminary call.

Bach-I hate the person who calls up and says we're having an opera fair in the Bronx, and we're offering you the woman who's putting it on. And I say that sounds a little narrow in appeal, and I can't visualize it. I tell the person it sounds a little boring, and I myself would tune it out. And she says she's a wonderful guest, wait till you meet her. Well, that's no good. I don't know that the woman has had a brilliant private life, or that she is witty and can tell jokes. This is the person who turns me off, the person that can't understand that I need some idea of how the interview is going to go. Another thing. People who send meaningless information, or so much information which is just boring to read, and doesn't tell you anything.

Goldberg-I would tell them to fake the fact that they don't have a professional public relations person working for them, and that they should make themselves sound like true professionals. Now this is my bias, and may not be valid. I do understand that it costs a lot of money to hire a professional, so if you don't have the money, make up a nice letterhead, and be articulate. Your book should be just what these people are looking for. This book is a great idea. I wish I had thought of it, Steve. Anyway, it's all in the approach. And I can't stand to be pressured, or when a person says, "well, can't I call back next week, after I give them a no." Learn to take no for an answer. And the press release. The press release should be creative, without being a phony. Ask some questions within the press release that you would assume an interviewer would ask.

Faris-Be honest and don't lie, because it will get you nowhere.

Koster-Never be afraid to try. Send information that gives full specifics on what you have. Be brief, and always put your name and phone number at the end, so that the story can be authenticated. Be as original as you can. So many people want publicity, so if you can outdo your competition with a clever and unique idea, you'll probably succeed. I remember a group that said all their members were going to dress in Bicentennial costumes, blah,blah, this and that, and they hyped it up as being really good. What it turned out to be was one or two people, dressed in costumes, and the rest dressed in shirts and shorts. When the photographer from our paper arrived and saw this, he refused to take a picture. He took one look and said no. They hyped us. Here we thought we were going to see the Revolutionary War, and all we saw were a bunch of guys running around in their undershirts. So this group lost the publicity they wanted because they ripped us off. Don't ever promise something that you are not going to have. If you expect five people, don't tell us you're going to have 1,000.

Salek-Write us a note with the idea, and we'll take it from there.

Wingo-We work under a very tight schedule with a relatively small staff, so we like to be told things briefly, quickly and cleanly. Information presented this way gives us the opportunity to make an initial reaction and say, "yes, we'd like to know more." This creates the opening for more information and dialogue on the subject.

DO YOU ENCOURAGE PEOPLE TO CONTACT YOU WITH THEIR IDEAS AND STORIES?

Price-Oh, sure I do. We're always looking for fresh ideas.

O'Brien-Always.

Barrett- By all means. We always want new ideas and material.

Nagle-Yes, we take phone calls all the time.

Franklin-Sure. I'm open to all ideas and guests.

Spalding-NBC is the largest news gathering organization in the world. We are flooded with information. If someone has an idea, great. That's what we're here for.

Bach-I like everybody to make a stab. If they are able to convince me it's a good idea, then we're off and running.

Goldberg-I always do. Publicity people can really help you out. We help each other.

Faris-Yes, anytime.

Koster-Very much. Especially something that would make an interesting feature story or picture. A story about a guy 95 years old, who still goes to a gym regularly to work out, would make an interesting story and an interesting picture. A story about a person who maybe had a severe medical problem and triumphed over it is a good story, but not a good picture. Many papers don't like to use pictures of handicapped people, and sensational looking poses, because they think it's yellow

104

journalism, pure sensationalism. O.K., that would make a good story, but not a good picture. Then you have, let's say, kids making something for the Bicentennial. That's a good picture, but not a good story, but under the picture there would be a few lines explaining what the picture is about.

Salek-Yes, and we depend on it.

Wingo-We welcome it. We look for the best material we can print, and never want to have a blind eye to anything. We're always open to ideas from anyone.

HOW DO YOU PREFER PEOPLE TO APPROACH YOU? SHOULD THEY CALL FIRST WITH THEIR STORY, OR PUT THEIR IDEA IN WRITING?

Price-Basically, I find that when people call me and tell me what the idea is, I can tell them quickly whether I want it, and I can give an immediate yes or no. It saves everybody a lot of time.

O'Brien-If they call, I can give them an immediate yes or no, and tell them if they should pursue the matter. But since we are so busy here, I prefer a person to write first with their ideas.

Barrett-Put it in writing, and give us at least three days to look over the material.

Nagle-Put it in writing first, and then call us the day you want the story covered. I plan my show day by day. Sometimes, we'll do a story and hold it on the shelf, and later fit it in another day's show. But usually it's a day by day thing.

Franklin-It's always better in writing. It gives me a chance to look over the material.

Spalding- Call first, and if I'm interested we'll take it from there.

Bach-A phone call is the way most people prefer to do it.

Goldberg-I don't really care, even though sometimes I'd rather not hear the phone ring. Sometimes you really can't listen, and more than likely, I'll say send it to me anyway. This way I get a chance to look at the information at my leisure and re-read it later. It's much more helpful to present your case on paper. A phone call may not be remembered.

106

Faris-Usually, someone with a story idea will call up. That's the initial approach.

Koster-Either way.

Salek-It's more effective to write a note. Editors and staff writers tend to get very busy. I don't think a telephone call is as effective as a letter because if you catch a person at a bad time or bad day, no matter how good your story is, they'll either put you off, or say they're not interested, or they don't have the time for it. But if it's in black and white, and it arrives in the mail, if the editor is too busy when receiving it, he'll set it aside and get to it another day.

Wingo-Always put it in writing. The telephone is the most evil instrument ever created. Initially, anything anybody has to suggest to me has to be on paper, preferably less than a page. That is the beginning. We can move from there.

WHAT TYPE OF WRITTEN INFORMATION SHOULD THE PERSON SEND?

Price-Besides background information, I need a plan, let's say a 15-point plan, which lists interesting ideas or topics we can get into. This way I can see clearly what we can do with the guest on the show.

O'Brien-Most important is a brief letter listing about 10 key story points. A picture and other related information is helpful, too.

Barrett-A release and biography are terribly important. Suggested questions are helpful. The type of information someone should send, though, depends greatly on the guest.

Nagle-Material that is self-explanatory and concise. Many times we'll just say go when talking to a person, if interested in the idea, and when they do give us information, we need their name and phone number. This is the most important thing, in case we have to reconfirm or we run into problems, we will know who to call, and have a phone number.

Franklin-Just a fact sheet, release or biography will usually do. Long letters and piles of information never get read.

Spalding-A brief synopsis about the idea, and also the person's name and phone number so I know who to contact. Also the date when the person is available for an interview. So a release and contact number are the most important. Also, a little letter if the person called originally, to remind me of our conversation, and that here is the material that I asked them for.

Bach-Brief information with a socko point. Something that will catch my interest.

Goldberg-The release is important. It must be creative, and packed with information. It can't sound like a soapsuds commercial. Also, send me background information, a bio, and if it's an idea, give me a history of how this idea came about. I need facts. But the release usually convinces me.

Faris-People must be able to convey their message on paper as well as they do verbally, and they must write simply. They should put themselves in the reporter's seat, and read it back to themselves. They should ask themselves, is it a lie, or informative? A person should try to be different. We get tons of stuff in the mail every day, so if we get something that's different, and to the point, already this person has scored five points out of 10.

Koster-At least a release with the five W's, who, what, where, why and when. Who it's going to be, what it's going to be, where it's going to be, why it's being done, and when it's going to be.

Salek-A one page release, keeping it as brief and concise as possible. It should be neat, typed, and preferably triple-spaced. A publicity person can get tips from any newspaper on proper style simply by calling and asking. Most newspapers have a little brochure which tells how to write a release or simple news story. This can help anybody who is a publicity director for their club, group or organization. Let's say somebody is publicity officer for the American Legion, okay? This person calls me up and says, "We are installing our officers next week. Can you do a story on it for us?" Well, I'm not going to turn that story over to a staff writer. I'll ask the person who called to please mail me the information. If it arrives, and is clean, and all it needs is to be edited, marked-up and a headline put on, it will get through in a snap and be printed. If it needs a rewrite, it's going to end up in a big pile for the rewrite person, and it will take a while. The news, in this case, the election of officers, might be very old news by the time it's rewritten and printed in the paper. So when a person wants a simple press release or announcement to appear in our paper, this person must write the story himself, and it should be neat and clean.

109

Wingo-If we are interested in this person, and this person fits into one of the various sections of our magazine...an adventurer, a doctor, a teacher, whatever, then I will get back in touch with that source and tell him we are interested. This is when we ask for as much background and written information as we can get. This is after we agree to cover the story.

HOW MUCH WEIGHT DOES THIS PRESS KIT CARRY? IS IT THE DETERMINING FACTOR AS TO WHETHER OR NOT YOU AGREE TO AN INTERVIEW?

Price-The press kit can be great, but I'm still going to pre-interview him. If he's not articulate, and does not have an energetic personality, I won't book him no matter how good his press kit is.

O'Brien-Yes. And the press kit should be neat and punchy. It should never be handwritten. It should be a simple and attractive package. I usually know after just readng the first sentence or two whether or not the guest will be used.

Barrett-The press kit should really grab someone's attention. Yes, it can be the determining factor. We're inundated with mail here. The smart publicity person will send a package which is attractive or unique. I'm more inclined, out of sheer curiousity, to read that press kit first. The opening paragraph of the release will either grab me, or turn me off.

Nagle-It varies. Usually we're sold on an idea before, when we first speak to someone on the phone.

Franklin-It's very important. The press kit, if well organized and prepared, shows that it's not just a matter to be taken lightly.

Spalding-You can't sell something until the person you speak with knows what it is you're selling. The press kit, then, is very important. It helps to sell an idea.

Bach-The final analysis rests with how interesting the guest is. You know that there are certain people who can come on and be great, and can talk about anything. There is a certain famous star, I don't know what she

111

can talk about to make her interesting. I don't know if this star is just hostile or what, but she lowers her voice, and is very stingy with her responses. You get a sort of yes and no. The first interview Arlene ever had with another star was a famous disaster, because he was shrugging his shoulders and looking at the ceiling, and gave barely audible answers. The last time we had him on, he was talking about all sorts of cosmic and philosophical things, and he was just terrific.

Goldberg-It either convinces you or it doesn't.

Faris-No. The determining factor would be when we've followed up and checked a story out. I'll then assign a reporter to get back in touch with the person if we're interested. Before we print a story, we must be sure it's true, or else we would be cheating our readers and giving them a bum steer.

Koster-If they're trying to sell me something that's pure balogna, no matter what they write, they won't sell me. The idea is most important, coupled with good written material.

Salek-If it's a typical release announcement, like electing officers, announcing a meeting, or something else along these lines, that's when the person seeking publicity does the work, and we expect him to write the story. If it's a feature story, that's when we want our staff reporter to work on it. On a feature story, background information about the story idea is important to us, but not an elaborate press kit. The idea is what's most important.

Wingo-Yes, and I can usually tell in the first three sentences whether it's somebody we want to do.

QUESTION 11

AFTER RECEIVING AND REVIEWING THE PRESS KIT, DO YOU USUALLY GET BACK IN TOUCH WITH THE SENDER, OR DO YOU RECOMMEND THEY CALL YOU BACK?

Price-It depends on how busy I am. If I'm really interested, I'll call somebody back immediately. I really try not to lead somebody on. Sometimes I might be interested in someone, and keep them on file for several months, until I can find an opening spot for them.

O'Brien-I will get back to them as fast as I can, or they can call me. But nothing turns me off more than the person who keeps calling and nags me.

Barrett-I prefer to call them back. You should always give the guest's availability date, so I know when I must reply by. If a person wants to call me back, wait at least three or four days after sending the information. This way I would have had a chance to review it.

Nagle-Give us a call, but don't nag. If you receive no response after calling once or twice, chances are we are probably not going to use the story.

Franklin- I don't usually have the time to call people back. I tell them to call me back. And if they want to get on the show badly enough, they do. Wait a few days to call, though.

Spalding-After the person sends me the press kit, he should wait a few days and then call me back. We're not remiss, but things keep piling up, so it's usually better for the person to call us back.

Bach-Every inquiry is answered. I don't mind at all if people call us back. By all means. They are entitled to an answer.

Goldberg-I'll get back in touch only if I'm interested. If he likes, the sender can call me back.

Faris-If I'm not interested in a story, I'll send a letter stating so.

Koster-If I'm going to do it, I'll call them. If you don't hear something, you might call back once, but if you make a pest out of yourself and call back every three or four hours, forget it. You can be sure the reporter will evade you.

Salek-We'll get back to the person after they send us information on a story idea, if we are interested. Then we'll assign a reporter.

Wingo-I answer everything. Wait for our response. I have a slow box and a fast box, but everything gets answered. Maybe not today, maybe not tomorrow, but eventually everything gets an answer.

DO YOU EVER DEMAND TO BE FIRST, OR HAVE AN EXCLUSIVE
ON A GUEST OR STORY?

Price-Yes, as often as we can.

O'Brien-When we were a network show, and on at night, and offered to fly a
guest in and pay his expenses, yes, we did. But now that we're
syndicated, no.

Barrett-Yes...and all other shows are monitored, so I encourage our guests
to be honest.

Nagle-Yes, on a major investigative story. Other times we request an
exclusive, but it's hard to demand something. It really depends on the
story.

Franklin-No, and I couldn't care less. I'd rather they go on all the other local
shows, because it gives me a chance to shine, and do something with
them that the other talk show hosts didn't do. On my show I deal
directly with the guest and ask about his life and background. Many talk
show hosts only ask their guests questions about current events, and
how they feel about problems in the community. Buddy Hackett told
me he preferred my way. Shirley Temple told me the same thing. So
have many others. Especially with celebrities and people in the public
eye. On other shows they're asked to comment on birth control, air
pollution, women's rights, etc. They never get around to the reasons
why a person became a celebrity, or an artist, or a doctor or businessman.

Spalding-No, we've never done that.

Bach- Since we are the top rated show, it stands to reason that it would be a dig for Arlene to take a guest after another show. I think that's generally understood and appreciated by everyone. I believe that this is one of the few shows where all the books are read, and all the research is done thoroughly. That helped to make us number one. The other day I was watching a TV show where Mrs. Jed McGruder was a guest. The host asked Mrs. McGruder if she thought her husband ever considered saying, yes, I did wrong. She looked at him startled, because that's what her book is all about. So he didn't read the book before interviewing her, and it seemed he never even picked up a newspaper. All he had to do was read the newspaper.

Goldberg-I can't do that because I'm only on weekly with my two hour program. My show isn't Midday Live, which is on every day, so I can't ask for an exclusive.

Faris-If it's possible, I do.

Koster-Only if it's a hard news story, like the first of a kind of story. If it's first, we want it first.

Salek-We do not.

Wingo-No. Our only concern is that we aren't picking up on something that has been used extensively in any other national publication.

HOW MUCH AIR TIME OR SPACE CAN A PERSON EXPECT TO GET FROM YOU?

Price-Maybe 10 minutes.

O'Brian- Each of our segments runs about 12 minutes.

Barrett-It depends. The minimum amount of time would be one segment, which is about eight minutes. If we're doing a theme show, the guest could stay on the entire 90 minutes.

Nagle-A feature story about one or two minutes. A major investigative story, longer. Generally, two minutes is the maximum you can really hope for.

Franklin-Depending on his achievements, about 15 or 20 minutes alone, and then he'll overlap with the rest of the panel.

Spalding-It's so unpredictable. We tape about 20 or 30 minutes, then we edit the tape and make about six or seven short features from it. These features run anywhere from a minute-10 seconds to two-and-a-half minutes. But I'd say most run one minute-10 seconds.

Bach-Around 45 minutes, with either a one-on-one interview, or a panel discussion with many people participating.

Goldberg-30 minutes, the most. I like to do panel shows with many guests.

Faris-If someone has invented the latest thing in pooper-scoopers, that idea won't cut that much ice at all. One paragraph to the pooper-scooper, and several pages for a major story. Again, it depends on the story.

Koster-With a photograph, a lot of space. If it's a feature story, maybe 200 words or more.

Salek-Anywhere from one paragraph up to a long, major feature. Also, we are on the mailing lists for all the networks, and our stories are used quite regularly on ABC. A story in our paper can give people additional publicity. The story I told you about before, about the boy who needed open-heart surgery, AP (Associated Press) picked it up from us. Then we had a story about a major restoration project that ABC picked up. There was a feature story about a telephone for the deaf which Eyewitness News picked up. The wire services and major networks can't be all places at all times, and rely very heavily on the local publications for stories and ideas. They have staffs that do nothing but read us. There's a gal at ABC who calls whenever she feels we have something of interest. This is how we all share, and how people can get additional publicity.

Wingo-One to four pages. Our stories are brief and sprinkled with pictures.

WHAT QUALITIES DOES A GOOD GUEST OR INTERVIEWEE
POSSESS? WHAT MAKES FOR A BAD GUEST OR INTERVIEW?

Price-A good guest has a good energy level and a somewhat pleasing
appearance, but the energy level is the most important thing, and how
articulate they are. And also very important is the quality of what they
have to say.

O'Brien-Originality, personality, integrity and taste, makes a good guest.

Barrett-A good guest must be articulate, compassionate and informative.
There are people who are worse than bad guests. These are the people
who are boring, not very knowledgeable about their subjects, and use
terminology which goes over the average viewer's head. In cases like
these, the viewer goes away with absolutely nothing but frustration.

Nagle-A person being interviewed has to have a good personality. He must
be emotionally involved in what he's doing, and give short, declarative
answers. The worst thing a person can do is disappoint us. A lot of time
and money is involved with sending out a crew to cover a story. So if
you say we should meet you somewhere, be there! If you say you will
have something with you, have it!

Franklin-The bad guest is the person who comes on the show only for
publicity. He knows publicity sells, and lackadaisically goes along, but
his heart and soul just isn't in it. That's the kind of guest who isn't
exactly exciting to me. I do understand that people want publicity. I'm
here to help, but in a case like this it behooves me to try and talk him up,
if he comes on like a sourpuss, acting like he's doing me a favor by
being on. And you want to know who the best guest is? He's the excited
one. The one who's animated, vivacious, and has something to say.

119

The one who doesn't try to steal the show by trying to relate every question to the title of his book, his name or his business.

Spalding-We dream of the guest who is going to be well spoken and articulate. Someone who doesn't "umm" and "uh" a lot while talking. It's so hard to edit that out. People who are self-conscious about their voices are hard to interview. If you get along fine in everyday conversation, you'll do fine in radio.

Bach-Some people are just dull. You sit next to them at dinner parties and can't get a spark out of them. A good guest should have energy, curiousity, chemistry, command of the language, enthusiasm and not too many giggles. It's really annoying to hear people make a remark they're a little embarrassed about, and then try to cover it up with a giggle or laugh.

Goldberg-This is an interesting question, because I don't get nervous doing interviews. It never occurred to me that people I'm interviewing may be nervous. That's very hard for me to understand. Even though they know their information, people who are nervous are the worst guests. There are also times when you do a bad interview. That makes for bad guests. If the interviewer is not prepared, or as sharp as he could be that day, there's trouble. If I'm distracted for some reason, you don't have a chance. A good guest must be relaxed and know his topic, and personality is just as important as subject matter.

Faris-Be articulate and talk in simple language. Be honest, because if you're not, you'll get caught. If someone tries to lie, we'll pick it up, because people aren't talking to dummies here. Experienced newspapermen are skeptical, and until the person truly convinces the reporter, there's always that little question mark in the back of his mind. If a reporter comes to me and says someone suggested a good story, but for some reason he has a little doubt about it, I'll tell him right away to drop the story. So above all, be honest. Also, I don't like people to pressure me. I work under pressure here all day, I don't need any more. On the other hand, if a person is too low-key, I may also be nesitant.

Koster-Politeness, frankness, and know what you're talking about. If you
don't know what you're talking about, you'll be in a lot of trouble.
Either you'll sound like a fool in the story, or the story will be dropped.
And if a person, for example, is a member of the American Nazi Party,
or a communist, and they make dumb statements, of course you're
going to make him up to be a yo-yo. But if the woman who is president of
the garden club doesn't know what she's talking about, the story will
probably be dropped, because no one really is going to try to nail her up
or expose her. One other point. If you want a reporter to list the 1,000
degrees which you hold, or something similar, don't try to recite them,
and make him sit there and write them down. Information like this
should be included in the press kit. Dishonesty, bluster, and intimida-
tion are the three worst things you can do. Don't be too wordy,and try to
take up too much of the guy's time. A reporter who covers a certain
town might have two or three other stories to do that night. So don't try
to take up more of his time than necessary.

Salek-A bad interviewee is one who only gives yes and no answers. A person
has to be willing to come across with the information, to be
knowledgeable about their subject, and be willing to impart that
knowledge to you. From that point on, it's up to the interviewer.

Wingo-The interviewee might be reticent, he may be bashful, he may be
secretive. Whether the interview succeeds or not is how adept and
professional the person is who is conducting the interview. You assume
in the beginning that the person is going to be worth your time, or you
wouldn't consider interviewing the person in the first place, that there is
something you want to know about the person, and if you don't get it,
it's your own fault.

121

CHAPTER 8

MEDIA LISTS

For those of you planning a national publicity campaign, I've included the following lists naming several of the many top national TV and radio shows, and newspaper and magazine publications, which can be utilized to reach your goals. Most are versatile in the choosing of guests, while others only cater to select interest groups or specific topics. Again, familiarize yourself with these shows and publications to see if they best serve your interests.

It would be impossible for me, for example in the case of magazines, to list every top-notch publication on the market today. If I attempted to do so, I would be able to write another book on just this information alone. Use my lists as a guideline, and then go to your local newsstand to check out other magazines which may be geared towards your particular interests.

Since contact names for each of these programs and publications change so often, it would be wise to first call (see Chapter 3) and find out with whom you should be dealing. If this is not possible, let's say you live too far from where the program or publication originates, then you should simply address your inquiries to "The Producer" (for a show), or to "The Editor" (for a publication).

123

How to Create Your Own Publicity

The lists which follow, I believe, represent the major and most sought after shows and publications of today, to be best used when seeking publicity on a national scale.

To the right of each named show and publication, I've left an area designated "notes." If you contact any of these shows or publications, use this space to keep an accurate record of what transpires. Also, make your own list of any local shows or papers contacted, to help you better remember and organize your publicity efforts.

TOP NETWORK AND SYNDICATED SHOWS
SEEN NATIONALLY

BOOK BEAT (PBS)   *NOTES*
WTTW-TV
5400 N. ST. LOUIS
CHICAGO, IL 60625

DAVID SUSSKIND (SYNDICATED)   *NOTES*
TALENT ASSOCIATES
747 THIRD AVE.
NEW YORK, NY 10017

DINAH (SYNDICATED)   *NOTES*
7800 BEVERLY BOULEVARD
LOS ANGLES, CA 90036

GOOD MORNING AMERICA (ABC)   *NOTES*
7 W. 66th STREET
NEW YORK, NY 10023

KUP'S SHOW (SYNDICATED)   *NOTES*
WMAQ-TV
MERCHANDISE MART
CHICAGO, IL 60654

MERV GRIFFIN (SYNDICATED)   *NOTES*
1735 N. VINE ST.
LOS ANGLES, CA 90028

MIKE DOUGLAS SHOW (SYNDICATED)   *NOTES*
INDEPENDENCE MALL EAST
PHILADELPHIA, PA 10106

PHIL DONAHUE SHOW (SYNDICATED)   *NOTES*
WGN-TV
2501 BRADLEY PLACE
CHICAGO, IL 60618

60 MINUTES (CBS)   *NOTES*
524 W. 57th STREET
NEW YORK, NY 10019

THE TONIGHT SHOW (NBC)   *NOTES*
NBC-TV
3000 W. ALAMEDA AVE.
LOS ANGLES, CA 91523

TODAY SHOW (NBC)   *NOTES*
30 ROCKEFELLER PLAZA
NEW YORK, NY 10020

TOMORROW SHOW (NBC)   *NOTES*
30 ROCKEFELLER PLAZA
NEW YORK, NY 10020

TO TELL THE TRUTH (SYNDICATED)   *NOTES*
375 PARK AVE.
NEW YORK, NY 10022

TOP RADIO—HEARD NATIONALLY

ASSOCIATED PRESS - AUDIO   *NOTES*
(CONTACT NEAREST OFFICE TO YOUR CITY)

127

DAILY PLANET   *NOTES*
149 CALIFORNIA ST.
SAN FRANCISCO, CA

NATIONAL PUBLIC RADIO   *NOTES*
2025 M ST.
WASHINGTON, D.C. 20036

PLNX (CBS)   *NOTES*
2020 M ST.
WASHINGTON, DC 20036

UNITED PRESS INTERNATIONAL - AUDIO   *NOTES*
(CONTACT NEAREST OFFICE TO YOUR CITY)

*TOP NEWSPAPERS/WIRE SERVICES
DISTRIBUTED NATIONALLY*

ASSOCIATED PRESS   *NOTES*
(CONTACT NEAREST OFFICE TO YOUR CITY)

UNITED PRESS INTERNATIONAL   *NOTES*
(CONTACT NEAREST OFFICE TO
YOUR CITY)

NORTH AMERICAN NEWSPAPER ALLIANCE   *NOTES*
220 E. 42nd ST.
NEW YORK, NY 10017

THE NATIONAL ENQUIRER   *NOTES*
LANTANA, FL 33462

  THE STAR   *NOTES*
730 3rd AVE.
NEW YORK, NY

UNITED FEATURES SYNDICATE   NOTES
220 E. 42nd ST.
NEW YORK, NY 10017

VARIETY   *NOTES*
154 W. 46th ST.
NEW YORK, NY 10036

TOP MAGAZINES—NATIONAL CIRCULATION

APARTMENT LIFE   *NOTES*
1716 LOCUST ST.
DES MOINES, IA 50336

BETTER HOMES & GARDENS   *NOTES*
1716 LOCUST AVE.
DES MOINES, IA 50336

BUSINESS WEEK   *NOTES*
1221 AVE. OF THE AMERICAS
NEW YORK, NY 10020

CHANGING TIMES   *NOTES*
1729 H ST., N.W.
WASHINGTON, D.C. 20006

COSMOPOLITIAN   *NOTES*
224 W. 57th ST.
NEW YORK, NY 10019

CUE
20 W. 43rd ST.
NEW YORK, NY 10036

NOTES

ESQUIRE
488 MADISON AVE.
NEW YORK, NY 10022

NOTES

FAMILY CIRCLE MAGAZINE
488 MADISON AVE.
NEW YORK, NY 10022

NOTES

FAMILY HEALTH
1271 AVE. OF THE AMERICAS
NEW YORK, NY 10020

NOTES

FIELD & STREAM
383 MADISON AVE.
NEW YORK, NY 10017

NOTES

FORBES MAGAZINE
60 FIFTH AVE.
NEW YORK, NY 10011

NOTES

FORTUNE   *NOTES*
1271 AVE. OF THE AMERICAS
NEW YORK, NY 10020

GOOD HOUSEKEEPING   *NOTES*
959 EIGHTH AVE.
NEW YORK, NY 10019

LADIES HOME JOURNAL   *NOTES*
641 LEXINGTON AVE.
NEW YORK, NY 10022

MC CALL'S MAGAZINE   *NOTES*
230 PARK AVE.
NEW YORK, NY 10017

MONEY   *NOTES*
1271 AVE. OF THE AMERICAS
NEW YORK, NY 10020

NEWSWEEK   *NOTES*
444 MADISON AVE.
NEW YORK, NY 10022

Media Lists

PARENTS' MAGAZINE   *NOTES*
52 VANDERBILT AVE.
NEW YORK, NY 10017

PEOPLE   *NOTES*
1271 AVE. OF THE AMERICAS
NEW YORK, NY 10020

PLAYBOY   *NOTES*
919 N. MICHIGAN AVE.
CHICAGO, IL 60611

PLAYGIRL   *NOTES*
1801 CENTURY PARK E., SUITE 2300
LOS ANGLES, CA 90067

POPULAR MECHANICS   *NOTES*
224 W. 57th ST.
NEW YORK, NY 10019

SEVENTEEN   *NOTES*
320 PARK AVE.
NEW YORK, NY 10022

SPORTS ILLUSTRATED   *NOTES*
1271 AVE. OF THE AMERICAS
NEW YORK, NY 10020

THE READER'S DIGEST   *NOTES*
PLEASANTVILLE, NY 10570

TIME   *NOTES*
1271 AVE. OF THE AMERICAS
NEW YORK, NY 10020

TV GUIDE   *NOTES*
RADNOR, PA 19088

U.S. NEWS AND WORLD REPORT   *NOTES*
2300 N ST., N.W.
WASHINGTON, D.C. 20037

WOMAN'S DAY   *NOTES*
1515 BROADWAY
NEW YORK, NY 10036

CONCLUSIONS—

TRACING THE STEPS TO SUCCESS

Now you know how easy it is to do your own publicity. Few people have had the opportunity to learn these trade secrets; the ones who have, have usually achieved the particular goal they were after. The process is simple, relying upon your own determination first, followed by the key steps revealed to you throughout this book. Top media professionals have told you their desire for information, it's now up to you.

I would like to summarize the key steps discussed in this book for getting free publicity. On the following pages you will find two checklists, each listing the most important steps to be followed when seeking publicity.

The first is for those of you who are business people, actors, writers, career professionals and the like, interested in planning a major publicity campaign.

The second list is for club or organization leaders, students and individuals wishing instant publicity for the purpose of promoting a single event or project, or for expressing an opinion.

Follow these checklists carefully. Check each completed step as you go along.

CHECKLIST NO. 1-THE MAJOR PUBLICITY CAMPAIGN

1. Develop your angle- Make sure your story or message will be of interest to other people.

2. Prepare your press kit- Your press kit should include the following:

   A. A release- a one or two-page story which tells about you or the idea you wish to publicize.

   B. A background sheet- a one-page list of additional important facts not already included in the release.

   C. Suggested questions- questions written by you about your subject for an interviewer to ask.

   D. Newspaper clips and photos- any newspaper or magazine articles which may have already been written about you will add to the credibility or importance of your story. Also, a photo of yourself adds personal warmth to your press kit.

3. Decide which TV and radio shows and which publications are for you, and which will best serve your interests.

4. Telephone those people responsible for booking interviews or guests and pitch them your idea.

5. Send your press kit to those contacts interested in you or your story.

6. A followup phone call, about a week later, should be made to make sure your press kit was received and reviewed.

Conclusions

7. Send a letter of confirmation to those contacts who agree to interview you.

8. Prepare an itinerary for your own use which lists names, times, addresses, dates and phone numbers of all your scheduled interviews.

CHECKLIST NO. 2- PUBLICITY QUICKIES

1. Prepare your press release- Some common types are releases which pertain to an event, an engagement, a birth, an anniversary, a club meeting, an exhibit, a fund raising benefit, an election of officers, or any other. Pictures may also be sent to accompany your story.

    A. Send your story to a newspaper at least one week before you wish it to appear.

    B. Limit your story to a maximum of two pages.

    C. Always type your release.

    D. Always double-space.

    E. Leave a one-inch margin on each side of page.

    F. Put your name, phone number and address on the release.

    G. Type the release date—the date you wish your story to appear.

    H. Type in the dateline- the city where the story has or will take place.

    I. Type in the lead- the first sentence of the story which usually runs only one sentence and tells the entire

138

Conclusions

story. The lead should answer the questions of who, what, where, why and when.

J. The remaining paragraphs in your release should list important story points which support the lead, in order of importance.

How to Create Your Own Publicity
The Following Publicity Ideas Are Optional-

1. Followup stories- Additional stories written which tell about the outcome of specific events already publicized.

2. A "letter to the Editor"-A letter sent to the editor's attention at a newspaper which voice's a reader's opinion on an issue.

3. Column items- Getting mention in specific newspaper columns which pertain to the idea you're publicizing.

4. TV and radio- public service announcements- Most TV and radio stations allow free air time to responsible individuals who wish to publicize a public service message.

5. TV and radio editorials- TV and radio stations will present opinions on controversial issues which reflect the views of the management at these stations. Viewers with differing opinions are offered free on-air rebuttal time.

6. Publicity stunts- Unusual stunts which you devise that will call added attention to you and your ideas.

7. Bulletin boards- Listing your announcements and events on community bulletin boards posted in stores, schools, churches and other public meeting places.

8. Cable TV- Getting on Cable TV shows which attract the audiences you wish to reach.

GOOD LUCK